Dow

FIFTY TO FOREVER

FIFTY TO FOREVER

Hugh Downs

THOMAS NELSON PUBLISHERS
Nashville Atlanta London Vancouver

Published in Nashville, Tennessee, by Thomas Nelson, Inc., Publishers, and distributed in Canada by Word Communications, Ltd., Richmond, British Columbia, and in the United Kingdom by Word (UK), Ltd., Milton Keynes, England.

Library of Congress information

Downs, Hugh.
    Fifty to forever / Hugh Downs.
        p.   cm.
    Includes bibliographical references and index.
    ISBN 0-8407-7786-8 (hc)
    1. Aged—Care—United States. 2. Adult children—United States. I. Title. II. Title: Fifty to forever.
HV1461.D68   1994
646.7′9—dc20   94-9259
                                                 CIP

Printed in the United States of America

1 2 3 4 5 6 7 - 00 99 98 97 96 95 94

To Michael and Sadie Shaheen
Milton and Edith Downs
who paved the way for us

CONTENTS

FOREWORD

There is no demographic count of the polymaths in America—those wonderful individuals who are extraordinarily open-minded, who love ideas and new knowledge, and who retain it, integrate it, and talk about it in interesting and provocative ways. Such a person is Hugh Downs, whose television persona is said to have been seen by more people than any other. Those who know Hugh Downs appreciate that he is a man of substance and personal loyalty possessing both encyclopedic knowledge and compassionate concern for his fellow men and women.

As one of the nation's great communicators, Hugh Downs has spoken and written about the subject of aging very effectively. He anchored, for example, the excellent Public Broadcasting System program "Over Easy"—a program about aging issues—for a number of years. Now he is making another contribution with *Fifty to Forever*. This book is lucid, encyclopedic, and compassionate. It is a needed, comprehensive guidebook for any of us who plan to grow old and who already may have older loved ones to take care of. It is loaded with solid information that is presented in Hugh Downs's always respectful and sensitive style.

This guidebook demolishes many of the stereotypes and misinformation about old age, older people, and various institutions that may serve them, and it points the way to effective old age. Hugh emphasizes the critical role of the family in the care of older relatives and the vital importance of letting older people take charge of their own lives. At the same time, he does not avoid the harsh realities of the most serious age-related disorders such as dementia and issues such as how to choose a nursing home. The appendix itself is a major resource covering such diverse topics as nutrition, fitness, finding help, and crime prevention.

America is growing older. Thirteen percent of our population is now over 65. The oldest Baby Boomers are now 48 and are beginning to experience the issues affecting their aging parents and grandparents. In two decades, these Baby Boomers will themselves be in old age, and some 20 percent—one out of every five Americans—will be 65 and older. As a society and as individuals, we must prepare for this impending change in the age structure of our country. Society must institute new policies and social arrangements and have a clearer vision of how to make the quality of late life as high as possible. Individuals must also revise their images of old age and play a vital part in securing a decent later life for themselves. The ability to do all this depends on having appropriate and useful knowledge at hand—the kind of knowledge contained in *Fifty to Forever*. Hugh Downs's book will do much to educate us all.

Robert N. Butler, M.D.
Brookdale Professor and Chairman
Department of Geriatrics and Adult Development
Mount Sinai School of Medicine

ACKNOWLEDGMENTS

All of us owe a debt to many heroes who have battled myth, prejudice, and injustice in matters of aging and eldercare for many years. A list of those who have affected my education and understanding would far exceed the space allotted, so I will here express my gratitude only to Dr. Robert N. Butler, head of the Department of Geriatrics at the Mount Sinai Medical Center; Dr. Harry R. Moody and Dr. Rose Dobrof, colleagues at the Brookdale Center on Aging at Hunter College; and Dr. Arthur Strimling of Hunter.

I would be remiss not to acknowledge the late U.S. Representative Claude Pepper of Florida for his constant, courageous struggles in legislative halls and other public arenas, which gave me hope for fairness.

I am grateful to Bob Slosser and aides Ruth Ford and Jaci Whitfield for their assistance with the manuscript and to Bruce Barbour, Lonnie Hull DuPont, and Sheryl Taylor for their skill and understanding. And without the friendship and wide-ranging knowledge of Peter Kunhardt, president of Kunhardt Productions, the project wouldn't have gotten off the ground. To Jean Ferrari, who made my clock and calendar comply with the demands of the project. And to my wife, Ruth, who kept me in line and who has been my core inspiration for fifty years.

INTRODUCTION

The purpose of this book is to help senior citizens and their families come to grips with the special accommodations and medical attention they may need in the years ahead. Most often the children of elders end up facing the issues of their parents' long-term care in crisis situations. And those issues strike fear in the hearts of young and elderly alike, conjuring up frightening images of senility, dying, and death.

What those children and loved ones need above all in those paralyzing situations is trustworthy information and advice—quickly.

My goal is to meet that need, to help people make swift and correct decisions, but more importantly to plan and prepare in a comprehensive way to produce the best of years, not the worst of years.

You Need Confidence

The primary thing I want to tell you, if you are one of those people, is this: you are probably far more capable of handling what's ahead than you think. It's possible you now see only pain, dislocation, and guilt—lots of guilt.

I want you to see your potential for strength, courage, and goodness, plus a good deal of humor. Your individual potential is huge.

First I will discuss general, attitudinal, even philosophical matters that are very important to elders as they face the future. And because they are so important to elders, they should be important to caregivers and potential caregivers who are trying to plan for the uncertainties ahead. I'm speaking specifically of steps that should be taken to keep seniors active and participating in life instead of being put on the shelf to deteriorate and lose, prematurely, the will to live. Closely related to that are the opportunities for improving and maintaining health conditions.

I will also discuss the increasing opportunities for home health care and adult day care, which so often make it possible for seniors to keep living in their own homes; this discussion will be followed by thorough exploration of the complexities of long-term care. And I will examine the host of questions raised by these matters: financial, legal, medical, insurance, and safety. I will also provide some practical directories of resources and checklists to make sure you've touched all the bases.

Lies Are Rampant

The best name for my overall subject is *eldercare*—to my mind a title that gets us away from pejorative word combinations discriminating against elders. Some years ago, I wrote a little book called *Thirty Dirty Lies About Old* in reaction to deplorable untruths thoughtlessly circulated about a simple little word—*old*. Those lies do terrible injustice to a valuable segment of our society which deserves, in my opinion, more respect and is more in need of justice than any other segment.

You might be interested in a sampling of those lies— still rampant, I'm sorry to say:

- Thinking slows down significantly as you age.

- Intelligence declines with age.

- All old people are wise.

- Old people need less (of everything).

- Old people die because they're old.

That last one is like saying "Young people are born because they're young." As a matter of fact, many prominent physicians will tell you that nobody ever died of old age. The causes are accident, disease, body abuse and wear-out, systems imbalance, organ failure, electrolyte depletion, etc., but never old age. And the other lies are just as bad.

The beauty of the word *eldercare* is its precision. It says exactly what it means without discrimination.

Words Are Important

Why do I make so much of this? Because discrimination against the elderly, like all discrimination, must be ended in this country and around the world. Elders are vulnerable and often left out. They have been left far behind in the "rights" parade (although they're gaining).

A good place to begin is with words, which almost always reflect attitudes. We need the kind of word campaign against misconceptions about seniors that the Surgeon General's office waged against cigarette smoking. As we'll see, merely throwing government money at the questions surrounding America's treatment of its seniors will not solve everything. But there is a role for government. It can and should help significantly, especially in creating awareness and helping set priorities.

Let's Change Assumptions

When we reach the point where society labels us *senior citizens,* we are wide open to dozens of stereotypes, largely based on our early assumptions regarding the aging process and its effect on people. We tend to assume that as we age we will customarily become forgetful, will suffer from pain and illness, and eventually will be forced to surrender our independence and move into an institution.

These things happen to people but not to everyone. The problems can in many cases be forestalled and in all cases be dealt with.

Four Kinds of Aging

In reality, there are four kinds of aging. The first, of course, is *chronological*. Every time my birthday rolls around on the calendar, I am forced to recognize that I am a year older. Chronological aging is implacable; it cannot be modified.

Then there is *primary physical aging,* which refers to my body's natural response to the fact that I'm posting more and more birthdays. The deterioration accompanying this response varies with individuals and lifestyles.

Beyond that, there is *secondary physical aging,* which occurs when physical aging process is accelerated by factors such as trauma, disease, poor diet, chemical abuse, stress, or exhaustion. We find we have a great deal of control over many of these factors.

But nationally, perhaps the saddest form of aging is what we can call *social aging*. This phenomenon asks society to believe certain myths about older people. It teaches deadly misconceptions. And tragically, many (or most) older people succumb to this viewpoint of themselves, and they behave accordingly. They wallow in false assumptions. What about you?

If It Says Old on the Label . . .

We inadvertently abet those negative assumptions by the actual words we use to refer to elders. Martin A.

Janis, who served as director of the Ohio Commission on Aging and as a member of the Advisory Council of the National Institute on Aging, noted a long list of popular labels, including *senior, senior citizen, oldster, older person, elderly, 65+ers,* and a few others. He suggested that *seasoned citizen* would be a better alternative.[1]

The late Helen Hayes preferred the term *maturian,* because "it says there's still a bit of fight in us." She explained that, in her opinion, the best part of recent history is that "the miracle of modern medicine prolongs health and life so that 'old' does not have to sound like a punishment."[2]

Norman Vincent Peale, the late American preacher of positive thinking, echoed the attitudes of many regarding those labels. "I'm one of those who is growing older," he wrote. "Come to think of it, who isn't? But some of us are now what they call 'elderly,' or senior citizens, neither of which terms much appeals to me personally. I've just always considered myself a man named Norman Vincent Peale. It happens that I've been around a long while. But so what? I'm the same person. Granted, I've experienced some physical changes, as do all older people, but that doesn't need to invalidate one's personality."[3]

At any rate, our accepted labels all seem to contribute to widespread misconceptions regarding aging. In our youth-oriented society, "old" people are commonly misrepresented as necessarily poverty-stricken, lonely, ailing, and inactive.

Evidence from Research

A survey commissioned by the National Council on Aging in 1974 demonstrated this way of thinking rather effectively. Pollster Louis Harris selected a sample of people ages 18 to 24 and asked them about their beliefs regarding the lives and life-styles of "older people." Here are some of the results:

- A full 62 percent felt older people have a "very serious problem" of not having enough money to live on.

- Almost the same number, 60 percent, believed that loneliness is a "very serious problem" for the elderly.

- A slim majority, 54 percent, said senior citizens suffer the "very serious problem" of not feeling needed.

- Just over half, 51 percent, reported a belief that the elderly have a "very serious problem" with poor health.

Granted, these problems do hit some elderly people, but they are not necessarily the norm, as revealed by the remainder of the study. For Harris also surveyed people 65 and older, and their answers gave a very different view of their lives, indeed showing the falsehood of prevailing assumptions:

- Only 15 percent reported a "very serious problem" with making ends meet.

- Twelve percent indicated a "very serious problem" with loneliness.

- Only 7 percent reported a "very serious problem" with not feeling needed.

- A total of 21 percent said they had a "very serious problem" with poor health.

Old Is Older Than Me

Although the Harris survey is twenty years old, the false images unquestionably persist. Eighty-one-year-old Sherwood Wirt addressed them in an opinion piece titled "I Don't Know What Old Is, but Old Is Older Than Me." He wrote: "Linking such terms as 'old' and 'feeble' is as out of date as 'horse' and 'buggy' or 'middy' and 'bloomers.' Don't lay us out in lavender yet; we are just as much alive and (in our own way) vigorous as anybody. In the 1990s we are not 'old folks' any more; we are simply folks who are older."[4]

Certainly we can hope, as our senior citizen population continues to increase, that more and more of these harmful stereotypes will be reexamined and found in error. Given the exponential growth within that population, perhaps we can count on that happening sooner rather than later.

Just think. In 1910 the average life expectancy in the United States was 52 years. Today in the Western industrialized world, life expectancy has climbed to 72 for men and 79 for women.

Longevity Revolution

In an effort to describe this trend, my friend Dr. Robert N. Butler, the first director of the National Institute on Aging and now head of the Department of Geriatrics at the Mount Sinai Medical Center, New York City, coined the term *Longevity Revolution*. This term is not overdrawn. About one of every eight Americans is age 65 or older, and the number is still increasing.

Along with that rise in longevity, we see an apparent increase in the overall health of our seniors. You could say we're not just getting older—we're getting better.

Some estimates indicate that Americans age 65 and older are averaging less than fifteen days a year in bed because of illness. This is a far cry from the diseased state that many would like to assume elders are forced to accept. Admittedly, Americans under age 65 have a lower average—less than six days a year in bed because of illness. But when you compare the figures, you must remember the effect of the small percentage of elders who are bedridden year-round. Their unfortunate circumstances greatly inflate the statistics. The indication, then, is that generally healthy seniors truly are healthy.[5]

As this gray-haired sector of society continues not only to grow but also to grow older and healthier, an interesting phenomenon is occurring. For decades we defined middle age as falling between 35 and 50. Since 1933, we have echoed Walter Pitkin's sentiment exhibited in the title of his book *Life Begins at Forty*. Today, however, because of medical advances, coupled with an increased awareness of nutrition, general health, and fitness, some biomedical scientists are actually defining middle age as falling somewhere between 50 and 70.

So there goes another popular myth. And as those misconceptions fall one by one, perhaps we finally will see the end of another negative assumption—that seniors will be forced to give up their independence and eventually require institutional care. Statistics simply do not support this myth.

The Dirty Lie About Nursing Homes

In reality, only about 5 percent of our population over age 65 lives in nursing homes at any one time. Furthermore, a cure for Alzheimer's disease would cut that number in half, emptying 50 percent of the nursing home beds currently occupied.[6]

Beyond these few who require institutional care, perhaps 15 to 20 percent suffer from a disabling illness or injury that may limit their independence but do not necessitate nursing home care. By simple mathematics, you can see that 75 to 80 percent of our elders are in relatively good health and able to function independently in society. In fact, many seniors are getting along just fine on their own. And for many others, a little extra effort on the part of relatives and friends will enable them to maintain their independence and live in their own homes indefinitely, or at least longer than most people think they can. I will discuss this further in Chapter 5.

Let's Do It

But now it's time to get on. I trust it's clear that this book will deal with eldercare—the myths, the problems, the fears, and the solutions. As I said at the beginning, most of you—whether seniors or their adult children—are more than competent to overcome the challenges ahead. Remember, some may never require the help we'll discuss; other elders may need extra help to stay in their homes, and still others may require institutional care as they become older and more frail.

The idea is to face the challenge, plan for it, and overcome it. So let's do it.

1

THE BEST WAY

Not everyone, I realize, is as fortunate as I am, with good health, stimulating work, and the perfect spouse. And good fortune is undeniably a factor here. The focus of this book, however, is on those elements outside the province of luck: risks that can be modified, actions that can be taken, attitudes that become self-fulfilling prophecies, and situations that can be exploited to maximize the pluses of aging.

Activity Is Crucial

I believe, therefore, that *active* is a crucial description for anyone desiring a full life, especially in the later years. To remove activity—and I'm not speaking of physical activity only—is to diminish life.

Activity is an important consideration as he or she, elder or loved one, addresses the future and eldercare.

As I said in the introduction, a crisis will have occurred in many cases before the question of long-term health care is properly discussed, and activity will have been displaced by mere survival. Accident, heart attack, stroke, advanced cancer, or any of a number of catastrophes will be in the driver's seat, at least temporarily.

Nonetheless, I'm obligated to emphasize this matter about which I feel so strongly as I begin to lay out plans and actions for you to consider for possible long-term health care. People, especially those advancing in years, must be encouraged (even pushed) not to allow themselves to be put on the shelf.

Society, sadly, has passed through decades of mandatory retirement and other indignities that label elders useless or over the hill no matter what the truth may be. And the truth is that usefulness and value have nothing to do with age. As I said in the introduction, old age never killed anyone, just as youth never caused anyone to be born.

The Forced Retirement Problem

Legal mandatory retirement has, happily, been set aside in most sectors of life, but the practice continues as policy in many corporations and agencies, causing me to shake my head at the unfairness and discrimination. I think of commercial airline pilots forced to retire at age 60 regardless of condition or qualification. Personally, I like to see gray hair in the cockpit in light of disasters apparently resulting from the inexperience and underqualification of younger pilots who were put in control.

It is a terrible waste of talent to force people out of their jobs only because of age. In fact, it is clear that in many cases mandatory retirement is from management's attempt to save money by hiring younger people with less seniority, often at the expense of the customer.

Stay Active When Possible

When possible, seniors and those who care for them should do everything possible to keep active—creatively active—in their regular jobs or perhaps second careers, community service, or hobbies. And industry needs to get behind this wisdom. It will be better off.

I recommend that we learn a lesson from the great, durable baseball pitcher Satchel Paige, who asked the profound question "How old would you be if you didn't know how old you was?" Satch didn't know how old he was, so he kept on pitching and striking out the younger folks in a long and winning career. We must give our elders that kind of atmosphere. They must not be forced or pressured to drop out; indeed, they must be strongly encouraged to do the opposite. It's a powerful way to fend off extensive long-term health care.

Attitude Is Important

I want to say to seniors who are looking ahead and to their children and other family members: Self-worth is a major ingredient in how you deal with getting older. Don't mistake me for Pollyana as I say this, but attitude is critical. What we think and say reflects that attitude. I'm not superstitious in this, but we must be intelligently optimistic about our prospects, both as individuals and as a nation.

We've made tremendous gains as a people in the last century. Growing old in America is a lot better than it was in 1900. People are living longer, and they're living with better health. As a result, we have had an amazing twenty-eight-year increase in life expectancy during the twentieth century. That nearly equals the increase over the preceding five thousand years.

Of course, there are still problems, and we've created new ones. Think of the sandwich generation of younger middle age people with dependent young adult children and with aging parents who now, or may soon, depend on them too. But we as individuals and as a nation can overcome these problems, which in one sense have grown out of our medical and nutritional success. They will require major decisions. Attitude will be critical in that process too.

In this chapter I'm talking about the attitude and the follow-through that will keep seniors active and contributing to their lives as well as to the lives of others. The word *contributing* is important. Many people require a broader purpose than a hobby offers; they want to accomplish something; they want to benefit someone else. That desire doesn't shut down at any particular age. And neither does the ability.

Outstanding People of Age

Think of how much poorer our culture would be had Pablo Casals or Andre Segovia been persuaded at age 65 to hang up his cello or guitar. We would have lost nearly thirty years of musical genius and beauty, not to mention the wisdom, wit, and charm of their lives.

Think of what would have been lost if Henri Matisse had continued in voluntary retirement in his sixties rather than returning to his art with a new burst of creativity, only to be bedridden by surgery when he was 71. But even then he refused to quit working, pouring out new forms and color almost to the day he died at age 85.[1]

Not all of us have artistic gifts, but many have skills and talents that are not diminished by longevity.

Think of Claude Pepper, a senator outrageously smeared in the horrible days of McCarthyism in the fifties and defeated for reelection, only to return to Washington in 1962 as a freshman in the House of Representatives at age 62. He went on, among many significant accomplishments, to become the irrepressible champion of American elders. With trifocal eyeglasses, twin hearing aids, a pacemaker, and an artificial heart valve, he served unmatchably into his nineties.[2]

In international public life, none can forget Winston Churchill, who served his nation in wide-ranging capacities, beginning as a young man and continuing through two terms as prime minister during crucial periods for his nation and the world. It is especially notable that he didn't become prime minister—in the early stages of World War II—until he was 66, serving from 1940 to 1945 and again from 1951 to 1955. Eighty-one when he stepped down, he continued as a prominent world figure until his death ten years later.

At still another level there is Mother Teresa. About her, little need be said. A successful teaching nun among the privileged of Calcutta until she was 40, she felt a new call and began a work among the destitute and desperate, the lepers, the cast-out babies in the forsaken slums of Calcutta that has been unmatched in modern times. At 49, at 58, and at 60, broadening the work to include other nations around the world, she pressed ahead unceasingly into her eighties despite ill health and pain. Age was never a hindrance.[3]

I Tried Retirement

In my case, I fell into retirement without much thought in 1971 when I left the "Today" show, figuring it would be nice not to hear the alarm at 4:15 every morning and to escape the rigors of daily broadcasting. I thought, quite loosely, of doing some specials and other forms of broadcasting, working irregularly. I would live in Arizona, teach, write, and do a lot of the things I'd wanted to do for some time. I didn't use the word *retirement* at first, but the press did, and I went along with it.

I did all of the things I mentioned. They were quite satisfying, but I suffered a letdown. I believe now that the sensible person doesn't ever retire; he or she just changes activities or occupations.

That's what I did, in a sense, moving back into scheduled television in 1976 with the "Over Easy" program for public television and then taking on "20/20" for ABC in 1978, which I've been doing ever since. I've also done the "Live from Lincoln Center" broadcasts for the Public Broadcasting System. All of these jobs have kept me on the move, but happily so. I've followed my own advice about staying active, and I hope that you will, too, even if you don't keep the same pace you once did.

I must say, though, that were I to leave broadcasting tomorrow (which I don't plan to do), I would have a dozen or more things I'd turn to, and a lot of the credit for that goes quite simply to the fact that I've been in broadcasting, which opened up a number of avenues of activity for me. But I would have to add the special upbringing that I had in a poor, but unusually creative and challenging, farm family in Ohio. Those facts alone would not let me stop working in one way or another. I find life too stimulating to do that.

Early Life Down on the Farm

I want to share a glimpse or two into my family home life. That's where the motivation to do things, to be inquisitive—to be active—came from. It represents the kind of motivation we Americans must consider as we face the eldercare challenges ahead. My jobs in broadcasting simply built on this.

My dad was unusual in several ways, sort of self-made. Coming himself from an Ohio farm family, he borrowed his brother's motorcycle at age 19 and started going to Columbus for concerts or operas. Not only did he have no background and no encouragement in that sort of thing, but his mother once said, "Please don't tell the neighbors what you do when you go to Columbus because they'll think you're odd." But that didn't stop him; the path was uphill, but he fought on.

That particular interest resulted, by the time I came along, in a home that was preoccupied with good music. No questions asked, we listened to the opera on the radio every Saturday afternoon. Furthermore, while getting ready for church each Sunday, Dad always had the radio tuned to chamber music. I confess that I had little interest in chamber music—it went with being dressed up and unable to play outside—but the years of listening took hold in my late twenties. I began to realize the intricacy and beauty of it and eventually recognized it, the string quartets especially, as the purest form of music created.

Things like that, from both Mom and Dad, make me aware that as far as motivation to interest and activity are concerned, I, in Newton's words, stand on the shoulders of giants. They were not about to be put on the shelf, and neither am I.

An Interest in Science

In another field, I remember as a five-year-old asking my father, undereducated and underprivileged, how far it is to the moon. And he told me—238,000 miles. It meant nothing to me, of course; I'm not sure I grasp the magnitude even now. But I can remember clearly that I was so flattered at being given a grown-up answer (an accurate one too) that I never forgot the figure—and I was pushed toward an undying interest in scientific matters.

I remember another point of curiosity, one most kids grapple with. I couldn't understand the old puzzle that asks, *If a tree falls in a forest and no one is there to hear it, is there a sound?* So I asked about it. Dad, feeding my interest, took the time to reply, in effect, that the matter depended on one's definition of sound. If sound is the creation in the air of sound waves, then there is sound even if there are no ears to hear it. But if the definition of sound is impingement on an eardrum and affecting the nerves so the brain senses it, then there is no sound if there are no ears nearby. Easy.

In like manner, he dispelled my youthful puzzlement about what would happen if an immovable object met an irresistible force. "Those are mutually exclusive terms," he said. "The very existence of an irresistible force means there can be no such thing as an immovable object, and vice versa." By making this clear to me, he seemed not merely a role model but a hero.

I loved—and still do—the worlds of science and

logic, thanks to the constantly expanding world of a laboring father and his delight in sharing it with his son. I was nurtured and challenged, expected always to be interested and active.

Mother and Literature

My mother naturally contributed weekly if not daily to this inquisitiveness, the best illustration involving literature. I'm not sure it was justified, but my mom was sometimes criticized by super-fastidious people as not keeping a very neat house. I remember her saying, "Fifty years from now, nobody will know what kind of a house I kept. But they will know that I read to my children." And that she did—Dickens, Mark Twain, Emerson, Tennyson.

She loved to read to us, always having reading sessions at bedtime. I remember *Huckleberry Finn*. When she read it to me, I thought it was a wonderfully rousing adventure. When I was about 25, I reread it and saw great depth that I hadn't perceived as a youngster. I read it again recently and saw what powerful social commentary it is. Because my mother read to me all the time, I was interested enough to keep going back to one of the great works and to learn more and more from it.

All of these things contributed, I suppose, to the kind of person I turned out to be. I'm determined, God willing, to stay curious and active and to avoid the shelf. The range of my curiosity is enormous and has made me something of a dilettante (perhaps the world champion). I plead guilty. I like to try everything or at least know something about everything. So I dabble in many fields. For me this produces quality of life.

Moving the South Pole

Probably the craziest-sounding thing I had an opportunity to do was to move the South Pole in 1982. Actually I repositioned the marker, which scientists had determined was off by about ten meters.

It was a remarkable experience that came, again, through broadcasting. I had worked for six years trying to get an expedition to the pole, and everything was set. I then read that scientists were going to reposition the marker, and when I was on the phone with the director of the National Science Foundation in Washington, I asked when they were going to do it. In December, he said, and I responded, only half seriously, that I was going to be there in December and asked, "Could I be the one who moves it?"

They called me back in about three weeks and said, "We talked to the scientists down there, and they think it would be a good idea."

So a film crew and I flew from Christ Church, New Zealand, to McMurdo Sound and camped in the facility there. On December 10 we flew in a Navy C-130 to the pole itself, where the temperature was 27 below, which they said was balmy for that location. It was almost summer; the solstice coming on December 20!

How strange it was. The sun was 23 degrees above the horizon, seemingly never higher or lower, moving counter-clockwise, ready to begin its descent on December 20 to pass below the horizon on March 20 and to leave behind six months of winter darkness, with temperatures of 125 degrees below zero.

Another thing I learned was that the ceremonial South Pole, marked by a barber pole ringed by the flags of the treaty nations, is almost half a mile from the real pole position. A polar space satellite has made possible the accuracy of today's markings.

I was struck by the fact that the pole is out in a field that looks like an Indiana prairie, flat as far as one can see. The South Pole itself is a bamboo pole about fifteen feet high, with a tattered green flag on top of it. And that's what I moved—I simply moved it to the right place—at 6:10 P.M. Eastern Standard Time, Friday, December 10, 1982.

Using calculations made earlier, I then walked a radius seven and a half feet up the Greenwich Meridian, which gave me a circumference on which I could walk around the world in twenty-four steps, each one in a different time zone. I was the first person to know I was really walking around the world since that was the most accurate marking of the pole.

Now that was all made possible by broadcasting, but it was especially sweet for someone who is curious and who had even by then moved into the senior citizen years.

The Fascination of Space

Another story that provided me an opportunity to keep going in the manner of Satchel Paige was coverage of the space shuttle program. I've been involved in space in a number of ways, but a special challenge came when I was tested on shuttle landings. I made five "landings" in the simulator in Houston, but only the last two came down without "crashing."

On the first one, I ran off the runway. On the next two I flared too soon and with no power to hang on—the plane is essentially a glider—I came down in excess of fifteen feet a second and blew the main gear. But capitalizing on my experience in gliders, I managed to execute the next two landings successfully. This experience was a thrill because the simulation seems very real; I felt as though I would hurt myself if I screwed up.

I had other space opportunities. After two years on the board and a year as vice president, I became president of the National Space Institute. Eventually, I served as board chairman. When the institute evolved into the National Space Society, I became head of the Board of Governors.

These positions provided wonderful opportunities to get inside the space program—to submit projects to NASA and to have some impact on policy. I later served as an advisor to NASA. One thing about which I have become certain: a strong space program is good for the nation in many ways, providing, among other things, jobs that positively impact the economy.

Churchill:
Work, Humor, Longevity

Evidence suggests that Winston Churchill, like Milton Berle (Chapter 2), owed his active longevity in part to work and humor.

Britain's great World War II prime minister, who didn't attain the post until he was 66, saw and voiced humor in the most trying situations. In the early dark days of the war, in the midst of some of history's most moving exhortations, he seized the moment for irony in a radio broadcast: "We are waiting for the long-promised invasion. So are the fishes."

About the Laborite who ousted him as leader of Britain near the end of World War II, Churchill's wit was especially barbed. Among several stories, he quipped once that "an empty limousine pulled up and out stepped Clement Attlee."

A man who elevated language to weapon or delight, Churchill frequently jousted with the purists who stultified it. My favorite quotation came in a story about those who demanded that one should never end a sentence with a preposition. He concocted a sentence about a little boy who said to his mother, "What did you bring that book you're reading to me out of up here for?"

His humor seemed somehow to counter-balance habits that continually broke all health rules. He drank wine for breakfast when he wanted and champagne, brandy, and whiskey in significant quantities throughout the day. He smoked cigars endlessly. And he never exercised. His weight was excessive. Yet for most of his life his vitality was enormous.

Think of it: he was prime minister from 1940 to 1945 and again from 1951 to 1955. He was a member of parliament for sixty years, occupied all Cabinet posts but one, wrote more than two dozen books and hundreds of newspaper articles, remained solidly informed and vocal about world affairs, painted, and puttered.

He died in his ninety-first year.

A Love for Aircraft

It's not as cosmic as the space effort, but I have been able to maintain my love for ordinary aircraft, too, thanks in large part to broadcasting. In addition to the glider craft, which I really enjoy, I've had an ongoing fascination with propeller planes, especially the older classics of World Wars I and II. Eighteen years ago Cliff Robertson and I started a project of equipping our bi-planes (we each had DeHavilland Tiger Moths) with machine gun housings carrying 8mm cameras for dog-fighting. We both got too busy to complete the project.

But in 1992 I went to Atlanta to engage in a dog-fight with two T-34A fighters armed with laser guns. The planes were rigged with smoke flares so that when the laser beam hit certain sensors in the other plane, a kill was clearly registered by the release of a lot of smoke. One of the aficionados of this hobby was 75 years old, a veteran of World War II. There is no age at which one has to stop playing.

The More Artistic Activities

The love for music fostered so many years ago in my childhood down on the farm has never waned; rather, it has increased. While I studied piano, violin, and classi-cal guitar, I never fully mastered any instrument. But I became a real virtuoso on the phonograph, listening for a couple hours a day on average.

I also got into composing along the way, and I am

currently challenged by a cello piece I'm working on for the remarkable Yo-Yo Ma. I've been very fortunate to have some of my work performed by full orchestra as well as smaller groups. I even have found myself captivated enough to try my hand at pop and country.

Education Is Important

I further believe that everyone must stay open to education, formal and informal, no matter what his or her age. Acting on this belief, I went back to school in the 1950s for courses in cosmology at Columbia. In the 1980s, to satisfy my deep interest in gerontology and later in geriatric medicine, I entered programs at Hunter College, taking advantage of night classes, tutorials, and supervised reading. In 1986, I received a post master's certificate in gerontology. In 1992, I received a special certificate from Mount Sinai Hospital in geriatric medicine.

I doubt my education will ever be completed. And it seems to me I learn faster and more efficiently the older I get.

We're Never Too Old

The point I want to make with these examples is that age alone cannot disqualify us from learning or from contributing to life around us and thus to our own life. But I'm afraid many of us need convincing on the matter. We too quickly let custom, prejudice, lethargy, or misunderstanding disqualify us and put us on the shelf, where it is certain that we will wither. A functioning mind keeps a mind functioning. Often, the same is true of a physical body. So with all my strength, I want to encourage all of you—elders, children of elders, society in general—to embrace activity and participation for seniors. Everyone needs it.

Perhaps one day our culture will progress to the stage found in Nepal, which I've visited several times. There, upon meeting strangers, it is the polite thing to ask how old they are, which would raise a few eyebrows in America. There, someone fifty would probably speak apologetically and say, "I'm only fifty." Whereupon the inquirer might say, "Oh, don't feel bad. You're getting there."

To call someone old is a compliment in Nepal. Wouldn't that be great? Solomon had it right when he said, "The silver-haired head is a crown of glory."[4]

2

IT'S OFF TO WORK WE GO

You seniors reading this book may be nodding your heads in agreement about the importance of staying active, while you know in your hearts that there is more to what I'm saying than meets the eye. There are obstacles to continuing to work, for example, and they're not only within you. I want to talk about overcoming those obstacles.

Milton Berle's Secret

I remember the unpredictable time—funny yet serious—when I interviewed Milton Berle on "20/20" in 1984. He said, "The secret to looking young at 76 is: I travel around with much older people."

That may be an appropriate, if humorous, step toward *looking* young—youth by comparison. But what about *feeling* young? Feeling young requires an infinitely more complex answer built on a variety of factors, not the least of which is a feeling of self-worth, which I noted before. Staying involved and active is one of the primary ingredients of that feeling. It is one of life's greatest elixirs. Don't let retirement ruin it.

I'm talking primarily to elders here, but their encouragers—their families—need to hear it too.

The venerable "Uncle Miltie" agrees with this attitude about activity, as he showed while speaking to a group at a senior center. "Don't make your bed your home," he said, "because there are a lot of people that like to stay in bed—not from being tired, but, like, I have nothing to do and I'm all alone."

Berle's true secret to aging gracefully is a twofold prescription—humor and work. "Laughter is a very imperative thing," he said. "I think it takes away much stress from people. . . . It relaxes them."

Researchers seem to agree. Some point to the physiological value of humor and laughter to the nervous system, circulatory system, respiratory system, and skeletal and muscular systems.[1]

And as far as staying busy? "I know a lot of guys that retired in their forties, and they became old men when they were 46," Berle told me. "I think that's the secret to the longevity of a person . . . to keep active all the time. Get a hobby, save stamps, do something, and keep busy."

It's Not Always Easy

Certainly Berle gave a wise admonition to me and my viewers, and he has earned the right to speak on the topic. But beyond recognizing that we should stay active, many of us are faced with a very real question. How does an elder who is either retired or moving toward retirement do that? It's one thing for people like me to keep saying, "Stay active! Stay active!" Sometimes it may not be so easy to accomplish. Where are the jobs?

Few are as fortunate, for example, as the Rt. Rev. Robert B. Gooden, Episcopal Bishop of Los Angeles Diocese some years ago. When he reached the age of 100, he offered to retire from his diocese. But his superiors rejected his resignation, saying he was still alert, capable, and in fact irreplaceable.[2]

But for those who have retired, particularly those who have been *forced* to retire, maintaining an active lifestyle may be a considerable challenge. How do you stay involved in life if retirement has robbed you of your sole outlet for creative energy and, perhaps, for social contact?

The first move probably is to find a new job or embark on a second career. Admittedly, it may be difficult to find a job you like, but you may find that the results are well worth the effort.

Bob Hope Works Hard and Loves It

*W*hen I was president of the National Space Institute and we were planning a fund-raising dinner in Dallas for the Werner Von Braun Fund, someone said, "Why don't you call up Bob Hope and see if he'll come?" A performance by Hope obviously would do wonders for such an event, so I reluctantly called and asked, almost apologetically, if he would be able to come.

"Just a minute," he said. "I'll have to look at my calendar."

He went away for a few moments and then picked up, "Sure, I'm free. I'll come down." He did, and the dinner was a major success.

That incident and others like it convince me that Hope, now in his 90's, does not see himself as having accumulated a lot of years; he just loves to work, has a great capacity for it, and keeps on.

Research for this book has made obvious the thread running through the lives of those who have stayed active well into elderhood. I believe the thread is attitude and work. Many ask, "Are they healthy and active because of their attitude or do they have a good attitude, because they are healthy and active?" I believe attitude is the beginning, followed by activity, followed by health—assuming an absence of serious accident or disease.

I believe we see this in the continuation of Bob Hope's amazing attitude and manner as found in the wonderful, carefree "Road" pictures with Bing Crosby many decades ago. It never occurred to him to stop.

The Benefits

One obvious benefit to finding a job or moving into a second career is the increase in income. Some experts say the income of the average retired person drops to one-third of that brought in by an employed person age 55 to 64.[3] If you find yourself in that situation, you may be looking at employment opportunities for very practical reasons. I would encourage you, though, to contact your local Social Security office to find out how much you can earn without endangering your benefits.

But even beyond the practicalities of increasing your income, you may find a job that you really enjoy. In that situation, work can provide

- A schedule for daily living;

- A sense of purpose and productivity;

- Physical and mental stimulation;

- Opportunities for social contact.

The Place to Begin

Your state employment agency is a good place to begin a job search. It charges no fee, and you may even find it has a special department for senior citizens. The office should provide free employment counseling, and the staff might also refer you to training programs in your area.

I don't necessarily recommend private employment

agencies because they tend to charge high fees, and frequently they do little more than keep your résumé on file. This is especially true for senior citizens. You may find an exception in your area, particularly if you run across an agency that specializes in finding work for senior citizens. There are a few agencies that do that. But regardless, you will want to research thoroughly the track record of any agency before you pay a fee or sign a contract.

Temporary employment agencies, on the other hand, may be a wonderful alternative. They offer flexibility in your work schedule. They provide a much better chance of finding work. And generally, they charge no fee because you become their employee. You can find temporary employment agencies in the yellow pages of your local telephone directory.

Even beyond these suggestions, check out the resources in your community. Call your YMCA or YWCA. Many of them offer job counseling and placement assistance.

Your local Area Agency on Aging also may have arrangements with businesses and organizations interested in hiring retirees. If you can't find the "Triple A" listed in your telephone directory, you may want to call the Eldercare Locator at 1-800-677-1116. The representative who answers should be able to tell you how to reach the Area Agency on Aging closest to you. Or call the National Association of Area Agencies on Aging at 202-296-8130. Or consult Appendix B of this book to find the unit of aging that serves your state. A phone call to this agency should help you track down the Area Agency on Aging closest to you.

And don't forget about your church or house of worship. Many congregations are responding to the economic hardships of unemployment by starting their own job networks. They keep lists of business people from within their own fellowships, particularly those who have employment needs. Then they match those job openings with qualified people in the congregation who need employment. You may find a position that is exactly what you want simply by calling the clergy or the secretary at your church. And if you find that your church doesn't offer this service, you may want to suggest it as an avenue of outreach.

Training Programs

A couple of federal programs offer help in training and placing senior citizens who need employment. The **Job Training Partnership Act (JTPA)** provides one source. Most of the funding to states under Title IIA of this act goes to local service delivery areas. It is earmarked for job training services to eligible individuals, including older workers (age 55 and up). In addition, a certain percentage of the annual allocation is reserved specifically to serve economically disadvantaged older workers. For specific information, including eligibility requirements, contact your local Area Agency on Aging.

Also, the **Senior Community Service Employ-**

ment Program (SCSEP) is a federally funded program designed specifically for individuals over the age of 55 living at subpoverty income levels. The program offers training and placement in twenty-hour-per-week jobs at places like day-care centers, schools, hospitals, and senior centers. If you are interested in additional information about this program, look for the Senior Community Service Employment Program listed in your local telephone directory.

Through the SCSEP, you may discover programs like Green Thumb, the nation's oldest and largest operator of employment and training programs for older Americans. Green Thumb was founded in 1965 by the National Farmers Union as part of President Lyndon Johnson's "War on Poverty." Beginning with 280 participants in four states, Green Thumb was originally designed to put older rural Americans to work beautifying our nation's parks and highways.

Now Green Thumb enrolls more than 18,000 older Americans in forty-four states and Puerto Rico. Its participants are involved in a variety of community service tasks such as tutoring, teaching skills and crafts, providing home health care or day care, and preparing and delivering meals for the homebound. They also work as clerks, mechanics, and laborers. They operate computers and do much more.

Women may find additional help through the National Displaced Homemakers Network. This organization defines a displaced homemaker as a woman who has "lost her primary financial support through widowhood, divorce, separation, a husband's long-term unemployment or disability, or the discontinuation of public assistance."

The network offers support groups, career exploration, advocacy, job training, job banks, counseling, tuition assistance, and many other services. For additional information, contact the National Displaced Homemakers Network at 1625 K Street, NW, Suite 300, Washington, DC 20006, or call 202-467-NDHN(6346).

In addition to these resources, you may want to check with your local YMCA or the Salvation Army. Organizations like these may offer training programs. Your local office of the American Association of Retired Persons (AARP) is another good source of information. And I'm sure if you brainstorm, you'll come up with some other resources unique to your locality.

Self-employment

Some retirees feel as if they have worked all their lives for someone else. They may need some extra cash to make ends meet, or to continue living in the style to which they have become accustomed. Or perhaps they simply aren't ready to resign from the sense of accomplishment and self-worth they gained through working. But neither are they ready to resume the rat race they just escaped. They want to work, but they want to be independent.

If you fit that category, perhaps you should consider

the possibilities of self-employment. You may not realize it yet, but you probably have some good ideas that could be marketed and advertised into a lucrative business.

Colonel Sanders Did It

Consider, for example, Colonel Sanders. Almost everyone has heard of him. But did you know that he started Kentucky Fried Chicken after retiring from another job?

The Colonel was an amateur cook, and fried chicken was his specialty. So when he retired at 65, he used part of his first Social Security check of $105 to take a stab at marketing his recipe. Eight years later he sold his business, logo, and recipe for $4 million, continuing to be paid as a promoter and consultant.[4]

I'm not saying you will necessarily achieve that level of success, but I do want to remind you that it's not wise to sell yourself short.

Other Possibilities

Cooking and/or catering is only one possibility for a second career. Suppose, for instance, that you have developed an avid interest in local history. Perhaps you could become a "house historian," offering new homeowners the opportunity to discover the historical relevance of the house they just bought.

Suppose you have become adept at a handicraft that

you always considered just a hobby. Perhaps you have developed a talent for photography (no pun intended). Or maybe you enjoy calligraphy or needlepoint or building birdhouses. You might be able to make money from your hobby.

Or suppose you have an idea for a unique service that is perfect for your local area—a grocery shopping service or a house-sitting or pet-sitting service. What can you do to take this beyond the idea stage? How do you make it a reality?

Research

The first step is research. Again, be certain that you check with your local Social Security office to see how much you can earn without endangering any of your benefits.

Then I suggest that you go to your public library to find information that will help you stay on the right track. Keep in mind that, according to some estimates, half of the small businesses in the United States fail within the first year, and 80 percent fail within five years.[5] That statistic doesn't doom you to failure. It just means you need to research and plan carefully for future success.

Evaluate Your Idea

Regardless of whether you are trying to market an idea or a service, or to open a store or business, there are some points you should consider to evaluate your idea.

Do you have any business experience? If you do, you're a step ahead in this process. If you don't, that doesn't mean you shouldn't continue to pursue your project. It probably does mean, though, that you need to educate yourself concerning the ins and outs of running a business.

Do you have a marketable skill or idea, and is it needed or wanted in your locality? What are general business conditions in your area?

Analyze how much you want to make and how much capital you need to start out. How long will it take for your income to surpass your expenses? And where will you get the capital for your investment?

Think about practical considerations. Where will you locate your business? There are advantages and disadvantages to working in your home. And for some businesses, particularly retail stores or restaurants, location may be a key factor in your success or failure.

Legalities

All things considered, you would be wise to obtain legal advice, particularly if you intend to form a partnership or corporation. An attorney or legal counselor can guide you through the myriad regulations that affect you.

For instance, if you *do* decide to work from your home, you will want to check zoning ordinances to make sure you can comply. Also, if you intend to make, package, and sell food items, keep in mind that this type of business is subject to many regulations at the federal, state, and local levels. And in some localities, you will need to register your business name and/or your product name at the county or state level.

Advertising

In the midst of all of your planning, don't forget about advertising. You may want to seek the guidance of a professional in the advertising field, but if money is tight, brainstorm and use your ingenuity. What advertising possibilities exist in your own community?

Don't overlook the value of demonstrations at civic clubs, samples in retail stores, interviews in your local newspaper or on the radio or television, and announcements on public bulletin boards. And an inexpensive but well-designed brochure is an excellent advertising tool.

Specific Information

I am able only to offer general information and to tell you of some areas that deserve research. Again, I suggest that you begin your research at the public library. You should find a host of resources to guide you through the process of starting a business and to help you plan for success. Beyond that, don't be afraid to consult experts. And, as I said, you may need an attorney to help you wade through the legalities. You may need an accountant to help you with the details of record keeping.

You may even be able to obtain practical advice through your local bank. Regional offices of the Small Business Administration provide another resource (a listing is included in Appendix F), as do university evaluation centers and entrepreneur centers.

Beyond that, you'd be wise to get in touch with the development agency in your county or city for additional information on how to contact those agencies. Just make sure you do your research and your preparation. It will help to turn your potential into reality.

Opportunities to Volunteer

Perhaps you aren't interested in working at all. Perhaps you don't want to risk endangering your Social Security benefits. Or you simply enjoy the freedom of retirement. But you aren't ready to give up on an active life. You want to stay involved. Don't lose heart. Hundreds of organizations across the United States need you.

And beyond the obvious benefits of volunteering, you may find that it improves your health. A recent study brought forth interesting facts about 3,000 volunteers: 95 percent of them enjoyed increased optimism and decreased chronic pain, apparently as a result of volunteering.[6]

Most hospitals and nursing homes would welcome

the offer of a volunteer to help with a variety of activities. Other organizations that seek volunteers include the American Red Cross and the Salvation Army. And don't forget public and private schools and day-care centers, political parties, churches and religious organizations, and civic clubs. Almost any nonprofit organization will not only find a place for you but also welcome you wholeheartedly.

Of course, the federal government funds several volunteer programs through the Older American Volunteer Programs, under the umbrella organization of AC-TION. Some of these volunteer programs are designed specifically for senior citizens while others encourage seniors to participate with people of other age groups.

The **Retired Senior Volunteer Program (RSVP)** is one such alternative. It places retirees age 60 and older in community-based organizations such as schools, museums, libraries, and hospices. They serve without pay, but they are reimbursed for out-of-pocket expenses such as transportation. Find RSVP listed in your telephone directory, or contact your local Area Agency on Aging for additional details.

Also, retired businessmen and businesswomen may be interested in the **Service Corps of Retired Executives (SCORE).** These volunteers help owners of small businesses or community groups that need their management expertise. The group is co-sponsored by the Small Business Administration (SBA). For additional information, you can contact the regional office of the SBA. When you call or write, you may want to ask about the **Active Corps of Executives (ACE),** which the SBA also sponsors.

Finally, older citizens are welcome to participate in **Volunteers in Service to America (VISTA)** or in the **Peace Corps.** VISTA workers help with programs that combat hunger, illiteracy, drug abuse, and child abuse across the United States. Volunteers must be at least 18 years old, but there is no upper age limit. VISTA recruits volunteers for one year of service from within the community where they will work.

The Peace Corps has welcomed older Americans ever since it began in 1961. The Corps asks volunteers to serve for two years in a developing country.

A Breathtaking Experience

Dorothy Burns Kelly, who joined the Peace Corps when she was in her sixties, was sent to a small village in the bush country of Sierra Leone, in war-torn West Africa. "It was an incredible challenge and a breathtaking experience," she told her hometown newspaper. "You have stories to tell your grandchildren forever. I thought I was going to save the world . . . but I discovered if you can change one thing, you make a difference."

After her two-year stint, Kelly returned to the United States, and now she works as a Peace Corps recruiter. "It's very competitive today," she said. But she added, "We get over 177,000 inquiries every year, and 15,000 people send in applications. Out of those, we take only 3,000."

But don't let that discourage you. She noted that "now the countries want people with specific skills as well as experience in areas like science, math, and agriculture. It's not just for kids right out of college anymore."[7]

For further information about the Peace Corps, you can call the agency's toll free phone number at 1-800-551-2215. For information about other federal volunteer programs, contact Older American Volunteer Programs, ACTION, 1100 Vermont Ave., NW, Washington, DC 20525.

Educational Opportunities

In the effort to stay involved in life, don't overlook the benefits of education. You will recall that while approaching senior citizen status rapidly, I returned to college to study gerontology, and it was one of the best decisions I ever made. (My education is not over yet. There are other things I intend to study when I have more time.)

More and more colleges and universities are encouraging seniors to enroll in classes. You can apply for college credit, perhaps even to finish a degree you started when you were younger, or you may want to alleviate the pressure of performance by auditing classes simply for fun.

Many schools also offer continuing education

classes. You can make arrangements through the admissions department of your chosen college or university. And don't forget to ask if the school offers reduced fees for senior citizens.

In addition to the courses offered at local colleges, you may be interested in educational opportunities designed specifically for senior citizens. One of the most widely recognized and recommended programs is **Elderhostel.** It networks colleges, universities, and environmental education centers all over the U.S. and the world. It offers week-long classes in fields such as literature and economics. Elderhostel catalogs are available at public libraries across the nation.

For additional information, you can contact Elderhostel at 75 Federal Street, Boston, MA 02110-1941. Elderhostel asks that you request literature through the mail. If, however, you have specific questions, you may want to call the organization at 617-426-7788.

Don't Assume You're Too Old

I have suggested a number of avenues that will help you stay involved in life. Regardless of whether you choose one of these alternatives or find a new one that is uniquely yours, don't let anyone convince you that you're too old to keep trying.

Consider the example of S. I. Hayakawa. In the 1976 elections, Hayakawa, then age 70, won the Republican senatorial nomination in California. He had spent most of his life as an academician and had little political experience. Furthermore, he had been registered as a Democrat until three years before he ran for office.

As you probably can guess, the age question came up during his campaign. Hayakawa responded, "Before World War II in Japan they killed off all the older politicians. All that were left were the . . . fools who attacked Pearl Harbor. I think that this country needs older statesmen too."

Apparently the voters agreed. Hayakawa easily won the senate seat over the incumbent, who was only 42 years old.[8]

Hayakawa's comment should not be applied only to statesmen. I think this country needs older teachers, executives, lawyers, secretaries, doctors and nurses, social workers, pilots, and volunteers. Don't ever let anyone convince you that you're too old to make a difference.

3

TAKING CHARGE

I'm addressing this chapter to elders, but family and caregivers should read it too.

You're the Key to Health

Your doctor, assuming that you have one, is a professional with years of training and presumably with years of experience and access to the most current information and techniques of the age. He or she is an important factor in your hopes for a long, healthy life. But he or she is not the *most* important factor. *You* are.

Most of us need to get that truth into our thinking and conduct. You are the key to maintaining your health throughout your life. And that means you must get involved and stop hanging back on the fringe, waiting for someone else to call the shots.

I'm not advocating disrespect or anarchy. Most doctors understand this. They know that ultimately you must act while they advise.

My Dad's Case

My dad was a perfect example of this principle. For a while as a widower, he let someone else make the decisions, and he lethargically followed along, coping the best he could with his understandable grief. He was taking blood pressure medicine. This particular medicine was really obsolete but still on the market, and some doctors still prescribed it. It threw him into confusion and pseudo-dementia, and the doctor prescribed tranquilizers and other chemicals to combat the condition. He became a yo-yo, between ten o'clock and two o'clock riding on a high that resembled intoxication and then falling into a low that caused an almost suicidal depression after the medication wore off.

Seeing him, my wife and I said almost simultaneously, "Good grief, we've got to rescue this man. He's dying right before our eyes." He seemed to be senile when he wasn't senile at all. A layman could easily have mistakenly interpreted the symptoms as signs of Alzheimer's disease.

So we encouraged him to go to a doctor in our area, who put him on more modern medication, and we saw a change almost immediately, again right before our eyes.

It was then that Dad began to take hold of his case himself. The conventional wisdom was that his new medication worked and he would stay on it for the rest of his life. But Dad, getting perkier, had no intention of staying on a medication for the rest of his life if he didn't have to. He changed his diet—a typical Mid-western one that included such things as fried steak and pan gravy—and began to emphasize lightly cooked vegetables and fruit, staying away from too much salt and refined sugar.

Taking charge, he monitored his blood pressure monthly with the local fire station's paramedic unit. As the pressure came down, he reduced the medication (with his doctor's guidance) until finally he stopped the medication and his pressure remained that of a 45 year old. He enjoyed almost ten more years of work and activity.

I trust the point is clear. The will to get off medication, when coupled with the will to take up serious preventive medicine, can sometimes produce really wonderful results. A top gerontologist acknowledged in a conversation with me some years ago, "We are beginning to find that out."

The Norman Cousins Story

My dad's experience offers just one example of an individual who changed his health situation by taking charge. Perhaps you remember another case involving Norman Cousins, who edited *Saturday Review* for more than a quarter of a century.

Cousins, who also served American society as a social critic and a free-lance international peace ambassador, endured a serious illness in 1964. It began with a slight fever and general achiness that eventually made it difficult for him to move his limbs and neck. The diagnosis revealed he was suffering from a serious collagen disease that affected his connective tissue. When the disease was at its worst, Cousins reached the point where his jaws were virtually locked together. The pain was severe.

So, in partnership with his doctors, he took charge of the situation. Some may see his recovery program as somewhat avant garde, and indeed, it did raise some eyebrows when he talked about it publicly.

At any rate, Cousins went off all pain medication. Then he checked himself into a motel room with a projector and a variety of old comic movies. He discovered that ten minutes of true laughter was a tremendous pain reliever; it allowed him to sleep for two to three hours at a time. He wrote a book about this titled *The Man Who Laughed Himself Well*.

Cousins coupled his "laughter therapy" with extremely high doses of vitamin C. His research indicated vitamin C would increase the production of his adrenal glands, essential in combating diseases such as arthritis, which falls into the same category as his illness. He emphasized that his symptoms did not immediately disappear, but eventually he became completely pain-free and regained his mobility.

Later, Cousins summarized his experience, writing that "a sharing of responsibility with one's physician is in the best interest of both physician and patient. The physician brings his or her trained knowledge; the patient brings a healthy system that needs to be freed to do its job."[1]

Norman Cousins was not, of course, immortal. Who is? He died in 1990, but I believe his attitude and actions gave him many years of quality life he would not otherwise have had.

The Aging Process

It's helpful to know some facts about the aging process as you learn to take charge of your health. For starters, aging takes place throughout life, being responsible in the early years for the body's growth and maturity. In the middle teen years it brings changes in the circulatory system, and, shortly after puberty, certain gland activity slows to a stop (or we would grow to be thirty feet tall).

The brain and central nervous system reach a peak of computer efficiency in the late twenties. In the thirties, skin elasticity begins to diminish; in the early forties, most people require reading glasses; and at different times for different people, hair follicles stop putting out pigment—and sometimes hair—with some people turning gray in their twenties and others not until quite late in life.

Margins Get Thinner

Eventually these and other changes bring some decline in capabilities and the abuse the body will accept.

Margins of effectiveness do get thinner. Still there are no hard-and-fast formulas about what changes actually take place, to what degree, at what rate, and how long they can be postponed with effort.

We can define physical aging as the body's increasing inability to adapt to the external environment and to adjust its internal functions. But age itself is not fatal, as I've said. Weakening of body systems with advancing years can increase the chance of disease overwhelming and ending life, and one may die of heart disease, cancer, stroke, or the like, but not of age itself.

The Baltimore Study

Studies about aging continue to challenge and refute prejudices about physical and mental abilities that have long influenced the treatment of older Americans, and yet the prejudices persist.

One of the studies that attracted attention was the Baltimore Longitudinal Study of Aging, a federally funded program examining the aging process in 800 men and women over several decades. The study, begun in the 1950s, included volunteers from age 20 to age 103 who reported each year or two for three days of tests. The results for each person were then compared with his or her own test performances of previous years, so that scientists could see a pattern of aging in individuals over time.

Some big changes in the common wisdom came forth. For example, while all standard graphs indicated that kidney function declined steadily with age, some subjects in the Baltimore study showed improved kidney function with time. The study challenged other misconceptions as well.

No Established Timetable for Aging

The aging process itself has no established timetable. Many physical functions change so slightly during a lifetime as to have little or no practical effect upon daily affairs. The effect of other changes can frequently be neutralized for quite awhile by modern medicine and technology and by personal determination to overcome whatever obstacles arise.

Young and *old* are simply words to describe the amount of time one has lived. You may well have been old at forty, but that doesn't mean you can't grow younger now. After all, how many of us feel as well as we *could* feel? You are better off being a fifty-five year old in top condition than a thirty-five year old who has let himself fall apart. A loss of physical and mental abilities can occur at any time of life, not just in the elder years. And failing fitness is not necessarily irreversible. Age can mean rejuvenation, or changing your life-style.

Become Informed

A good starting point for taking control of your health and beginning to affect it positively, as my father did, is to acquire information. Obviously, it's not something you can just play at; to do it, you must get and stay informed on preventive medicine. Your physician may be too busy with acutely sick people to spend much time coaching you. But you can become an informed consumer and get abreast of the state of knowledge in preventive medicine, which has been growing rapidly. A good place to start getting reliable information is the National Institute on Aging, which is part of the National Institutes of Health (see Appendix D).

When Something Goes Wrong

It is equally important that you know what to do when something goes wrong with your body. Remember, you will not be capable of curing all your ailments yourself or second-guessing your doctor's advice. But here are three ways you can become an informed consumer of medicine:

1. Understand when your condition is serious enough for you to call a doctor. Some patients rush to the phone about every ache and pain, making a nuisance of themselves. And some, out of ignorance and fear, wait beyond the time when they really need treatment. If you learn to recognize changes in your body and react appropriately, you will be at a great personal advantage.

2. Learn to communicate with your doctor about your condition so you can understand what is happening

and what the prescribed treatment is supposed to do. Accurate, clear description makes it easier for your doctor to diagnose your problem.

3. Learn to feel secure in your ability to cope with emergencies and try to take the right actions at the right time should anything go wrong. Illness is stressful in itself, but if you are knowledgeable about your makeup you can remove the mystery and fear and deal only with real problems.

If the partnership with your doctor is going to work, you will have to educate yourself medically to some extent. Happily, information about your own body makes fascinating reading, especially with the trend toward greater patient involvement.

Choose a Professional

Next in your involved, "take-charge" role is the responsibility to choose the professional or professionals who will care for you and with whom you must deal effectively. You need to feel confident about your family physician, since you will rely on his or her recommendations for specialists, testing, and facilities. Also retain your right to seek a second opinion if any doctor recommends or diagnoses something you really feel is not right. And get that second opinion independently of the doctor who rendered the first one.

You can choose either a family practitioner or an internist as a general family doctor. The former is like the general practitioner of times past but has done post-graduate work and should be certified by the American Board of Family Practice. An internist has trained in all areas of medicine except surgery, obstetrics, pediatrics, and geriatrics; he or she is ready to diagnose the common ailments of adults. An internist should be certified by the American Board of Internal Medicine.

Ways to Choose

How to choose? Start with your local hospital administrator, who can recommend staff members who practice in your area. Priding itself on its staff, a hospital strictly screens physicians wanting to practice there before granting affiliation.

The county medical society can also provide recommendations and specific information such as a doctor's hospital affiliations, board certifications, and alma mater. You can also ask dentists, lawyers, and other professionals, who will know the reputations of doctors in the area. Ask your neighborhood friends and any other sources you can think of.

If you're moving and need a new doctor, ask your present physician for recommendations. And you need more than a name. You need someone with whom you can establish rapport, a personal relationship that is open, trusting, and mutually respectful.

Points to Consider

You're looking for someone with whom you are comfortable in the following areas:

1. *Availability.* Your personal physician should have an office with convenient hours near your home. Find out who covers for him or her and check into the credentials and reputation of this doctor as well.

2. *Willingness to explain.* Your doctor is a busy professional, but it is essential that he or she be willing to take the time to explain to you what is wrong to the extent and in the detail you wish. He should let you know what he is doing about it, what medication or treatment he is prescribing, what you should expect, and what your options are. And you need the information in layman's terms.

3. *Willingness to accept consultations and second opinions.* Doctors are fallible. While you should certainly have enough confidence in your physician to accept his diagnosis of a routine ailment, you should also know that he can send you to an appropriate specialist when there is reason. If he is sensible, he will not object if you suggest that you would like to seek a second opinion in instances where you feel that the diagnosis is unwelcome or treatment has not progressed satisfactorily, or when the treatment he suggested is especially extensive.

4. *Reasonable fees.* Don't be embarrassed to ask the doctor what she charges. Doctors' fees vary considerably. You may want to investigate the availability of a health maintenance organization, which charges one fee for all your medical services.

5. *Compatible attitude.* There are many areas in which the doctor's personal opinions will substantially affect his or her medical decisions, so it is a good idea to find out where your doctor stands. Ask him how he feels about preventive medicine, and prepare a few specific questions on some aspect of nutrition or stress, to gain insight into his attitudes.

Ask About Your Doctor's Views on Elders

It is important also to determine your doctor's expectations for you as you grow older. If she's enthusiastic about your prospects, that's good, but if not, you may find that she will ignore or shrug off conditions she would treat in a younger person. *You* may understand that there is no reason for you to set low expectations because of age, but not every doctor recognizes that. Geriatrics, the medical study of aging, is still not widely taught in medical schools as it should be, but younger physicians are still likely to be more informed and more open-minded about elders.

Your Responsibilities

You have a number of responsibilities in the partnership you are trying to forge with your doctor. You are responsible for following his advice and dealing with him openly. It's also your responsibility to give him all the facts, including the circumstances that might be affecting your condition. This spirit should extend to paying your bills. Let the doctor know of difficulties you may have in paying, and try to work out an arrangement beforehand.

The Nutrition Factor

Another major component in any effort to take charge of your health is nutrition. It does little good—in fact, it may be harmful—to pursue health and fitness without reducing the dietary risk factors in your daily life. By making a few simple changes in nutritional habits, you (whether elder or younger) can improve your health now and help to ward off illness in the future.

It's hard for some to believe that simply eating whatever tastes good can jeopardize health. But many foods that have become staples in our busy way of life really aren't good for you. It is sad that many Americans still, after receiving so much information in recent years, prefer foods that are overprocessed, high in fat and calories, and low in nutritional value. But we're slowly turning this around and choosing the foods that will keep us healthy.

Over recent years, food manufacturers have realized there's money to be made by supporting better nutrition—or by convincing the public that they are doing so. Putting more healthful commercial brands with better nutrition labeling on the market is a step in the right direction, but it takes an informed consumer to set a nutritionally beneficial table. And if you want to succeed in taking charge of your own health, you need to become an informed consumer.

In Appendixes G and H of this book, I offer detailed plans for carrying out nutritional and fitness programs that will assist you in bringing your health under control as you move confidently into the elder years.

Remember Your Attitude

Learning about fitness and nutrition and developing a partnership with your doctor—these actions provide a great place to start taking charge. But there is one more item to consider.

Research indicates that attitude—a word I've emphasized many times already—is a more important factor in ensuring continued health than many people have realized.

The Centenarians

You may remember a "20/20" piece I did late in 1992 about a study performed by two Georgia professors named Leonard Poon and Gloria Clayton. Over a five-year period, they tested ninety-six independent, noninstitutionalized people who were at least 100 years old. They wanted to find the secret to long life.

Their discoveries were most interesting. The common thread could be summed up in one word: *attitude.*

Gloria Clayton explained, "We've uncovered four themes that exist among our entire sample, and those are optimism, engagement or commitment to something that they're interested in, activity or mobility, and the ability to adapt to loss."

On that program, we featured several centenarians who modeled those attitudes. Geneva McDaniel, 105 years old—whom we tracked down at a Grand Prix race for senior citizens—shared her secret with us.

"Well, think positive," she said. "Don't think negative. If you feel bad and you know there's something the matter with you, forget that and go and do what you have to do."

Continuing, we found that Jesse Champion, 102 years old, and his wife, Phronie, 85, were prime examples of people actively engaged or committed to something. In their case, the something was their religious faith.

I asked Mr. Champion if he was born again. "Yes sir," he said. "I know I've been born again. My hands look new. My feet look new. Yeah, he changed my heart. I had a hard heart, but he changed it."

Professor Clayton described Champion's commitment this way: "Rarely do they open the [church] door that he's not there, and I would venture a guess that no decision has been made in that church for years that he didn't participate in."

We found that Elva Spangenberg, 104 years old, had rejected the notion that *old* means *inactive*. She has maintained her interest in mobility and activity, even to the point of launching a new career at the age of 96. She had been working as a ticket seller at a local movie theater for forty years when the theater closed its doors for good. That very day, she was approached by the administrator at a historic mansion. "Didn't even give me a week off," she told me. She began working as a guide at the mansion immediately, and eight years later, she's still going strong. (The mansion, incidentally, was built when she was 6 years old.)

Ms. Spangenberg never married, but throughout her life, she was extremely close to her family, particularly her brother John. John had passed away almost forty years ago. In spite of her loss, Ms. Spangenberg was able to pick up the pieces. She retained her interest in life. She didn't give in.

Mary Elliott, 102 years old, is the same. Just one day before I was scheduled to interview her, Mrs. Elliott received the shattering news that her 77-year-old daughter had died. We sought to cancel the interview. But she was determined to go ahead, saying she would dishonor her daughter's memory if she let us down.

She recalled for me a time when her daughter was small. "I was carrying her back to her crib," she said, "and she lay down on the pillow, put her cheek on her hand, and she said, 'Now, dear God, let's go to sleep.' And she knew he'd be with her. And that made me think, as the morning progressed yesterday, in my state of shock, that I had been asked to give back to God the precious gift that he had given me, and just as quietly, just as beautifully." Mrs. Elliott has learned to adapt to loss.

What Does This Mean to You?

As I said, the four factors found in the research can be summed up in the word *attitude*. And your attitude toward aging can help ensure your continued health. If you accept the once-conventional wisdom that growing older only means getting sick, you will be defeated before you start. Despite what you may have been led to believe, the odds strongly favor your continued freedom from the kinds of health problems that would seriously limit your activities.

I've found dozens of vital, happy seniors across the country whose physical fitness is a key element in their busy life-styles. Not only are they busy with a number of work and service activities, as I discussed in the previous chapter, but they swim, golf, walk vigorously, work out in spas, and in general refuse to be consigned to the rocking chair. And they feel good about it in every way. They're in their sixties, seventies, eighties, and more, but they don't fulfill one of the most deeply ingrained and erroneous definitions of old age. Instead, they're active. They enjoy their bodies and what they can do with them and thrive on a busy life-style largely because they have taken charge of their condition. Being in shape lets them establish a way of life that keeps them in shape.

A majority of the seniors I've spoken with are pleasantly surprised at how well they feel. Frankly, many had not planned to feel well, but they're finding ways to take care of their most valuable asset.

As for those not yet in the elder category, they are reaping the benefits of having started to realize their possibilities while still in middle age. Let that be a word to you who are reading this book as you look ahead to becoming a caregiver. Begin now with your own health. Take the time to build a life-style based on healthful habits and maximize your own physical fitness as you progress toward elderhood. You and everyone around you will benefit.

4

A FAMILY
AFFAIR

Age has a way of sneaking up on all of us. As
J. B. Priestly, an English author, remarked, "It
was as though walking down Shaftesbury Avenue as a
fairly young man, I was suddenly kidnapped, rushed
into a theater and made to don the gray hair, the wrin-
kles, and the other attributes of age, then wheeled on-
stage."[1]

The First Recognition of Need

That first gray hair or wrinkle can be an unsettling
reminder of our mortality—and the reminders only increase with time. But, as disturbing as it is to deal with
the evidence of our own aging, it can be equally dis-
concerting to recognize that age has crept up on, and
perhaps caught up with, our parents or elderly relatives
and friends.

That recognition may come in a variety of ways.
Perhaps your mother will call to say she's just not up to

cooking Thanksgiving dinner for the whole family this year. Or perhaps your father's retirement will force you to face the fact that he's "not as young as he used to be." Regardless of how you discover that your parents are aging, you probably will begin to understand that they may need some help—if not in the near future, then in the distant future.

The Role of the Family

May I suggest that any "help" offered, if at all possible, should be a family affair. Aging truly impacts the entire family. One writer, outlining his own research as well as his experience in caring for his parents and in-laws, explained it this way: "If I have learned anything about old age, I have learned that it is a family time. Even in our pleasure-driven, divorce-and-forget society, children take care of their parents."[2]

And certainly it is true that, if additional help is required, the children are the most obvious source for assistance and support. My friend Val Halamandaris of the National Association for Home Care, believes that adult children have the ultimate responsibility to create a system that is most beneficial and most helpful to their elderly parents.

It seems most adult children agree. In fact, the whole idea that elderly parents are ignored by their children does not bear up well in the face of statistics. Some are being ignored, of course, and a few are even being abused. And it is true that the number of older parents living with their children has declined. Between 1957 and 1975, for instance, the percentage of older Americans living with their children dropped from 36 percent to 18 percent. But this change may reflect the improving economic conditions for the elderly brought about through Social Security and other financial support, which allow many to maintain their own homes.

The decline does not imply that a majority of adult children lack concern for their parents. A report in 1975 showed that three-quarters of the senior citizens in a survey lived either with their children or within thirty minutes of their children. More than half of them, 53 percent, had seen one of their children within one day of the interview, and 77 percent had seen one of their children within one week of the interview. Only 10 percent had not seen at least one of their children for a month or more.[3]

Although this data is twenty years old now, more recent research indicates the trend is continuing. For instance, a study by the General Accounting Office, cited in the June 1984 issue of a scholarly journal, supports this general finding. It noted that, even among the elderly who require a great deal of care, 80 percent of such care comes from relatives and friends.[4]

And a 1988 House of Representatives report supports this data as well, noting that the average American woman will spend seventeen years raising children and eighteen years helping aged parents.[5] I should note that while 75 percent of those caring for elderly adults are women, more and more men are shouldering this responsibility. And many of them are discovering the same thing I did: The benefits far outweigh the inconveniences.

Getting Organized

For anyone facing a situation where it seems to be necessary to start providing care for a parent, let me make some suggestions to facilitate the process.

To begin with, decisions regarding the care of your parents should be made within the family structure, *in concert with your parents*. Beyond this, it is crucial that you and your siblings coordinate your efforts and get organized. This will help to ensure that even while your parents are living independently in their own home their needs won't slip through the cracks.

I recommend that the family designate one person to be a *primary caregiver*. This person ultimately will be responsible if an emergency arises or if the parent is unable to make important decisions. The primary caregiver also will tend to any special needs for the parents' daily living.

The Problem of Choosing a Primary Caregiver

It is important to recognize that the process of choosing a primary caregiver won't necessarily be problem-free. In reality, every family is made up of unique individuals, each with unique talents, likes and dislikes, needs and ambitions, and personalities. Dealing with the necessities of caring for parents may strengthen relationships—perhaps even bringing healing for those teetering on the brink of dissolution. Or it may push the entire family toward civil war as it brings up unresolved arguments, conflicts, and differences of opinion, some of which may even be anchored in sibling rivalry left over from childhood.

Admittedly, you may not find it easy to deal with the stress and hostility that crops up in this process. If possible, though, it is wise to make important decisions regarding your parents' care, including the selection of a primary caregiver, as a family. And, of course, you should give priority consideration to your parents' wishes.

Possible Scenarios

The very best choice is a unanimous decision within the family regarding a primary caregiver for your parents, as well as a division of responsibilities among the whole group. But another possible scenario is that your parents simply will select a caregiver. This choice may be based on a conscious selection, or it may evolve over time, as your parents repeatedly call on one particular sibling for advice or help. Certainly, this is a viable option that may work out well for your family. But it may also breed discontent. It may prove to be an explosive situation if the adult children view this as a continuation of "playing favorites" that they believe occurred in their childhood.

At the other end of the spectrum, you may see one of the adult children, or perhaps an in-law, volunteer to assume this responsibility. Again, it may be a conscious decision, or it may simply have evolved over time. And yet, again, it may be a perfectly legitimate choice within your family structure.

Unfortunately, though, some families will have to deal with a "false caregiver"—someone who claims the title but doesn't do the work. Others will find their parents at the mercies of a "martyr caregiver"—someone who goes overboard with attention, even to the point of refusing help from other siblings, and then resents being left with the responsibility. Or, worse yet, some families may find their parents being used as a pawn in a power struggle among the siblings. (In a truly sordid scenario, the reward they hope for is a larger piece of the inheritance.[6]) I'm mentioning these dismal possibilities to help you resolve conflicts by understanding them.

I believe that when you recognize that your parents may need help, your best alternative is to call a family meeting. This option provides a forum for frank and open discussion of the issues involved in your specific situation.

Guiding Factors

Within the context of the family meeting, several factors may guide you and your parents and siblings in the choice of a primary caregiver. As I have already noted, women tend to be more likely to assume this role than men, but that isn't always true. Beyond the question of gender, perhaps one sibling will be a natural choice because she lives closest to your parents. This choice may prove to be especially beneficial if your family's goal is to help your parents continue to live independently. Or perhaps another sibling will be an obvious choice because of his personality or personal schedule.

Each family situation will be different, so you will need to work through this process in light of your family's mix of talents, abilities, locations, financial situations, schedules, and personalities. It is important, though, that the family not force anyone to assume this responsibility without offering that person the opportunity to analyze his or her ability to perform the necessary duties.

Later in this chapter, we'll cover some questions you should ask to determine your own capabilities as a primary caregiver. But for now, the recommendation is that you allow time for the selected caregiver to work through the issues involved in his or her own situation.

Denial

If you call a family meeting to discuss your parents' care, you need to be prepared for your parents, and perhaps your siblings as well, to deny the need for assistance. As I noted previously, it isn't particularly easy to admit that we see the effects of aging, either for ourselves or for our loved ones.

In the face of such denial, you have two options. You can "bide your time"—that is, wait and hope your parents or siblings will come to agree with you. The danger, of course, is the possibility of an accident or traumatic event that could be avoided through acting quickly on behalf of your parents.

Your second option is to forge ahead and explore the options on your own. Do your own research. This will enable you to offer viable options for care if your parents eventually face catastrophic illness or injury or if they simply come to admit they need a little help.

Try the Alternatives

You may even recommend that your parents try some alternatives just for a short period. Betty Ritter, a woman in Norfolk, Virginia, said she had been caring for her husband since he was diagnosed with Alzheimer's disease fourteen years ago. He balked at the idea of attending an adult day-care center. So she contracted for services for one month and convinced him just to try it.

"I cried for a week," she said. "I cried every time he got on the bus because I felt like I was deserting him."

But she soon recognized the benefit—to her and to her husband—for he loved his time at the center. He has been enjoying the activities there for almost seven years now.

You may find the same results with your parents, regardless of whether you are trying to interest them in adult day care or in some other service you feel could help. If they are willing to try it for a short time, they may come to appreciate the service and decide on their own that they want to continue using it. You won't even have to push.

Should You Be the Primary Caregiver?

If you are seriously considering the role of primary caregiver for yourself, I urge you to take stock of your situation before making the final decision. If you choose to accept this responsibility, you should know up front that you may face a variety of outside stresses.

You may experience pressure to "do the right thing." Well meaning people may remind you that, after all, your parents cared for you when you were a child. Now it's only fair that you should return the favor.

You may also encounter pressure caused by your parents' fear of institutionalization. Or you may endure criticism from other family members or "significant others" regarding the quality of care you are giving.

Yet, many times, those who criticize will be unwilling to offer additional help. You may also face added pressure if your spouse and/or children feel a need to compete for your attention.

Because of all these possibilities, I recommend that you examine your own motivations for accepting or refusing the assignment. What good reasons do you have to accept? What good reasons do you have to decline?

Second, I believe you should evaluate your relationship with your parents. Examine both the past and the present. Do you find unresolved conflict? How have all of you handled relational stress in the past? Whom do you think your parents would choose for a caregiver?

Keep in mind that negative answers to these questions do not necessarily mean you shouldn't become the caregiver. They may simply indicate that you and your parents need to work through some issues to increase the chances of this choice creating a good experience for everyone.

Third, look realistically at your personal situation. What are your current responsibilities and commitments? Which commitments cannot be surrendered or even changed? Evaluate your immediate family as well. Don't be afraid to ask questions. Do they understand what will be involved? Are they willing to support you? Are they willing to help you when you need them?

And fourth, as far as you are able, evaluate your parents' needs. Do they have any disabilities? List them and determine if those disabilities are repulsive or overwhelming to you. Be honest. You may even want to write your answers, because that will force you to put your feelings and attitudes into words. Consider calling your parents' physician to ask specific questions about their physical and/or mental condition. And as much as possible, ask the physician to look into the future. Can he or she give you an estimate of whether and how quickly your parents' condition will decline?

Granted, these questions only serve as a guide. They will not apply to every situation. Your parents may be in very good health. They may not need extensive care at all. But it is important that you keep in mind that situations change. There's a very real possibility that your parents' health will eventually decline. Answering questions like these may help you and your spouse and children to discuss the ramifications of your decision. Together, you need to plan for the present and for the future. Together, you need to decide what you can and can't do. You need to present this plan to your parents and siblings and get their input.

A Follow-up Meeting

You may want to ask for a follow-up meeting with your parents and siblings to outline the results of your personal evaluation. Be up-front and honest, and don't be afraid to ask for help. Remember that each sibling's contribution will vary according to relationship and geographic location. But even with that understanding, you may want to draw up some kind of informal written agreement to outline a plausible division of labor. Naturally, this agreement will depend on your parents' level of need. And it can be as specific as you all want, even including items such as financial support, food preparation, laundry, transportation, personal care, and medical treatment.

Some of this same information will be discussed in a later chapter regarding the decision-making process involved in having your parents move in with you. But it is important even at this point to recognize that caregiving can be very stressful, depending on the nature of your situation. It can drain you of emotional and physical resources. It can impact your immediate family. Certainly, siblings and friends should be sensitive to this fact. Help everyone involved to understand that *you* may need help.

Long-Distance Caregiving

Some of you must care for your parents from a distance. Or you may be exhausted and need a back-up caregiver. You may consider hiring a relatively new type of specialist called a care manager, or sometimes a case manager. These professionals are trained in social work, gerontology, nursing, medicine, or law. Their responsibility is to act as an advocate for the elderly client.

A care manager's tasks cover a broad range. He may simply oversee hospital stays, or he may manage long-term health care options in the patient's home. According to some estimates, as many as 75 percent of working care managers are hired by middle-age children who are trying to care for their parents from a distance.

Check the Credentials

Of course, you will want to check a care manager's credentials before you hire him or her. I suggest you find out how much experience this person has in geriatric care management. The following list provides a guide for the type of questions you will want to ask a care manager before you sign a contract or hire him or her by oral agreement:[7]

- Is he or she a member of a care managers' association?

- Does he or she have a professional license or certification for nursing or social work?

- Can he or she provide references from clients?

- Can he or she provide references from local hospitals or other caregiving facilities, or from the Area Agency on Aging?

- Will he or she arrange for free or low-cost or medically insured services when appropriate?

- Does he or she personally provide any of the necessary services for caregiving?

- Does he or she screen care providers?

- Is he or she affiliated with a caregiving agency? If so, what is the possibility that this person will check out rates from competing services?

- Is this individual insured or bonded?

- Who performs the necessary caregiving responsibilities when this person is off-duty?

- How often can you expect to receive reports concerning the condition of your elderly parent or friend?

- How much will this person charge, and what services are included in the fee?

- Will the private care manager provide a written contract outlining the specifics about fees and services?

For additional information and advice regarding this option for caring for your parents or elderly loved ones, you may want to contact your local Area Agency on Aging. (See Appendix B to find your state unit on aging. This agency can help you find the nearest Area Agency on Aging.) Or write to the National Association of Private Geriatric Care Managers, 655 N. Alvernon, Suite 108, Tucson, AZ 85711, or call 602-881-8008. If you send the staff of this organization a self-addressed stamped envelope, it will return to you a list of their members in your area.

5

HOME,
SWEET HOME

I trust that by now my conviction about independence for elders—working, health conditioning, overall living—has seeped into the tone of this book, but I want to get even more specific now.

Living as independently as possible is the best of all situations. And you should fight for it as long as it is reasonable for all involved.

People Want to Remain in Their Homes

Consider the positive aspects associated with this alternative. Beyond the satisfaction engendered in the senior who is able to maintain his self-sufficiency, some experts believe that having some personal control through living in his own home may actually add years to the senior's active life.

Dr. Butler notes, "There's no question but what people want to remain in their own homes as long as

possible. And having some mastery of your own fate—
some control over it—is actually found to be related to
the length of life that we will enjoy."

A Declaration for the Independent

For those who can manage very well on their own,
quiet support is still the best kind of help from relatives
and friends. You, relatives and friends, should reassure
them that they can depend on you if they need help.
Even though they may vehemently guard their independence, they probably want to know they can depend on you in a pinch. This is fairly easy, of course, as
long as they choose activities and behave in a manner
you approve. But what if they refuse to move out of a
neighborhood that you consider unsafe? Or what if
they start building friendships with people you don't
like or even approve of?

Frankly, your approval is probably inconsequential.
Your acceptance and dependability, however, are crucial. As long as a senior is able to make decisions and
choices regarding her present and future, she deserves
your support.

Of course, some "interference" may be necessary.
For instance, you may need to request a visit to the
doctor if your parent is suffering from a long-term illness and refuses to make the appointment himself. And
there are some warning signs that may indicate a gradual or even sudden loss of ability to make coherent

decisions or to perform necessary functions for daily living. We will cover them more extensively later in this chapter. But, in the meantime, a senior's independence and control—his feeling that he is the master of his own destiny, or at least that he has some say in the matter—is a precious commodity that deserves protection.[1]

Evaluating Your Parents' Position

Beyond that level of quiet support, one of the most loving things you can do for your parents is to help them take stock of their current situation and plan for the future. Consider their social needs, health care needs, and financial needs. While they are still in a position to care for themselves and to make rational choices and decisions, you can work with them to research the options for the future. Insufficient preparation places too many people in the intolerable position of making life-changing decisions in the midst of crisis situations involving illness or injury. Advanced planning ultimately will reduce stress if the time comes to act quickly on behalf of your elderly loved ones.

As I noted in the previous chapter, if they are emotionally unable to discuss potential problems, perhaps you should do your own research. This information will enable you to offer viable options if they should eventually face catastrophic illness or injury or if they simply need a little extra help.

Early Warning Signs

Absolute freedom and independence may become unwise and even unsafe. Primary caregivers should watch for and respond to early warning signs indicating that their parents need help.

For instance, what about *accidents?* Dame Edith Evans, who lived from 1885 to 1976, reportedly told someone, "When you fall down at my age, the great secret is not to try to get up too quickly. Just lie there. Have a look at the world from a different perspective."[2]

Unfortunately, for a lot of seniors accidents like that will not have such peaceful outcomes. According to the National Institute on Aging, people over 65 account for only 12 percent of the total population, yet they suffer 27 percent of all accidental deaths. And thousands more elderly individuals are severely injured in accidents each year.

It's only wise, then, to consider that an elderly person might need some additional help if he frequently suffers major, or even minor, accidents. It doesn't necessarily mean, though, that he has to move out of his house. He may be able to reduce accidents through some minor changes.

Look Through the House

Consider some simple changes in his home. Put yourself in his physical position, perhaps even using a walker or navigating in a wheelchair. Try to get around in his home.

Are the steps too narrow? Does she need a ramp? Are there area rugs that are easy to slip on? Are the door jambs a tripping hazard?

Meeting Eyesight Difficulties

Also consider changes that happen naturally with aging, and think about their effect on your parents. For instance, what about the loss of clear eyesight? For starters, if your parent isn't seeing as clearly as she used to, this could make it difficult for her to distinguish certain similar colors. It may affect her in various ways, such as hampering her ability to distinguish the edges of stairs, particularly if they are painted or carpeted with a dark color.

The answer to problems like these may be relatively simple. Mark the steps, or any other problem area like railings or corners, with brightly colored tape. Make sure the home is well lighted, but avoid glare. Use light bulbs that produce softened or diffused light. And reduce the glare from windows by using sheer curtains.[3]

Check the Bathroom Safety

It may also be wise to take a look at your parents' bathroom. Grab-bars in the shower or near the toilet can greatly reduce the difficulty of getting up and down or in and out. Applying rubber or adhesive strips to the bathtub or shower may prevent slipping. Some additional ideas for preventing various kinds of accidents are included in Appendix I.

Of course, there are other things to consider in this discussion. If your mother or father suddenly seems to be accident-prone, the trouble may have its root in physical weakness or dizziness and may require medical attention and advice.

Forgetfulness and Confusion

Forgetfulness and *general confusion* should also flash a yellow caution light to the primary caregiver.

Has your parent forgotten to turn off gas and electrical appliances in his home? Does he forget to take his medications? Does she mix up her dosages? When she wakes up from a nap, does she regularly forget if it's night or day? Are you noticing an increased use of or dependence on alcohol?

Watch for Depression

Depression may also become a problem. Some depression is natural. After all, it is fairly natural in people of all ages. And, for some people, old age is a time when they face loss of loved ones, loss of certain physical abilities, loss of familiar roles, and perhaps loss of financial security. A certain sense of mourning is normal in each of these situations.

Clinical depression, however, is something different. Extended and deep depression should be a warning sign for the primary caregiver. One major symptom of depression among elders is a desire to stay in bed all day.

Keep an Eye on Appearance

In addition to these other factors, the primary caregiver should be concerned about certain changes in the parent's *physical appearance.* You may notice a decline in personal hygiene or grooming habits. Or you may notice suddenly that she is losing weight. This may indicate she is no longer able to prepare meals, or it may mean that she has lost her appetite and food doesn't appeal to her anymore.

Don't Be a Lone Ranger

In the face of these and other warning signs, keep in mind that you are not required to play the Lone Ranger. Adult children do not necessarily have to fill these voids single-handedly. Many agencies and services exist to support the senior and help your parent maintain as much independence as possible.

Primarily these agencies fall into one category called "Home Health Care Services." This category includes services that are specifically related to medical supervision and care, such as visiting nurses, counselors, case managers, and physical or occupational therapists. But it also includes services that offer a more basic level of care, providing assistance with housework and general cleaning and maintenance, shopping, meal preparation, escort and transportation services, and personal companionship. I will list and describe some of these services later in the chapter.

In addition to helping your parents maintain independence, these services are beneficial in that they tend to be less expensive than nursing homes, and they can be tailored specifically to your parents' situation.

Help from Medicare

Medicare is a federal health insurance program under the direction of the Health Care Financing Administration (see Appendix C), but the Social Security Administration actually enrolls people for benefits.

Medicare is divided into two parts, labeled Part A (hospital insurance funded through taxes) and Part B (medical insurance funded through monthly premiums from enrollees). Although they cover different kinds of medical services and have different eligibility requirements, both cover some home health care needs.

In general, Medicare will pay for home health care only if the patient is confined to the home, though not necessarily bedridden, and needs part-time nursing care or therapy on the orders of a physician.

The home health agency that you choose must be certified by Medicare in order to qualify for coverage. Medicare enrollees may find they can be reimbursed up to 80 percent of the costs for certain medical equipment such as wheelchairs and hospital beds.

For specific information regarding your situation, contact your local Social Security office or call the Social Security Administration at 1-800-772-1213.

Medicaid

While Medicare is a federal program, Medicaid is a federally funded but state-run program designed primarily to help those with low incomes and limited resources. Therefore, benefits and eligibility requirements may vary from state to state.

For many patients, Medicaid will pay almost all costs for part-time nursing, homemaker-home health aide services, and medical supplies and equipment for those who meet eligibility requirements. However, the care provider must be certified by the state health department.

I recommend that you contact your local welfare or social service office for more information.

Assistance for Veterans

Some veterans, particularly those who need care for a service-related injury, may also obtain help through the Department of Veterans Affairs.

For additional information, you can contact the Veterans Administration hospital nearest to you or call the national headquarters at 1-800-827-1000.

Segovia Thrived on Genius, Work, and Wit

*A*ndrés Segovia, the master guitarist, who brought the instrument into classical respectability, continually exercised a dry wit, and lived long.

When he was 82, I attended a concert of his in San Francisco. The audience simply would not let him stop, relishing encore after encore. Finally, Segovia returned to the stage, guitar in hand, and spoke softly to his admirers.

"I could play for you all night," he said, "because I am young and vigorous. But the guitar is a fragile instrument, and needs its rest. This will be the last encore."

He told me that when he was a younger man, his relatives urged repeatedly that he visit a seer they respected. "He knows everything," they declared. Reluctantly, Segovia went. When he knocked at the seer's door, a voice came from inside: "Who is it?"

"I just left," Segovia said to me. "He didn't know everything."

I last interviewed the maestro in 1987, after attending his 94th birthday party in Madrid. On that occasion I learned that he had two natural sons, one a year older than I am, and the other a year younger than my grandson! In explaining this he said, "My friends say that I am prone to procreation."

As it turned out, Segovia died while we were editing the interview for airing. Deft editing and retracking some of the narration into past tense turned it into a memorial with a timeliness that surprised viewers.

Private Policies

Keep in mind also that some private long-term care insurance policies cover home health care. When you inquire about this possibility, make sure you check to see if a previous hospitalization or nursing home stay is required.

Older Americans Act

As a rule, nonmedical home health care services are not covered by government programs or private insurance companies. Federal programs under the Older Americans Act will provide some funding for home care and alternative long-term services. The Act is best known for providing nutrition services, but it may also fund home chore services and homemaker-health aides.

Also, check for resources within your own community or the community where your parents live. Many community organizations, religious groups, and civic clubs offer volunteer services free of charge.

Where to Get Specific Information

As I said, a general listing of home health care services follows in this chapter, and I hope it will define them more fully for you. Please refer to Appendix A for information about how to research the resources in your area. In keeping with this Appendix, for specific information regarding home health care services in your area or in the locality of your parents, I suggest that you call the Area Agency on Aging in that community. Again, if you cannot find your local Area Agency on Aging listed in your telephone directory, you can contact the National Association of Area Agencies on Aging at 202-296-8130. Or refer to Appendix B, which offers a list of state units on aging. If you call your state agency from this list, a representative there should be able to direct you to the nearest "Triple A."

Another excellent alternative for this type of research is the Eldercare Locator, a nationwide network of organizations serving older people at state and local levels. The Eldercare Locator can give information sources for a variety of services including home delivered meals, transportation, legal assistance, housing options, recreational and social opportunities, adult day care, senior citizen programs, and a host of other home health care options.

You can reach the Eldercare Locator through the National Association of Area Agencies on Aging, or by calling 1-800-677-1116. When you call, it will be helpful if you have this information ready: (1) the name and address of the senior citizen you are assisting (it is especially important to have the zip code, for this will enable the representative to identify the closest sources for assistance), and (2) a brief and general description of the type of assistance you seek.

Home Health Care Possibilities

Here is a general list of home health care services. I'll begin with those that are specifically related to medical supervision and move to the more general services.

Visiting Nurse Services

Your parent or elderly friend may be able to enjoy regular supervision of medical needs by a visiting nurse. The schedule of visits may vary as needed. Nurses can monitor medications. They can also track specific medical information such as blood pressure readings, and carry out certain medical procedures. In addition, they can offer advice about nutrition and general household management to make the living situation easier. Frequently, visiting nurses take a special interest in their patients, and the relationship provides a unique, personal outlet for the homebound. Medicare and Medicaid sometimes cover this type of treatment.

Homemaker-Home Health Aide Services

Often working in conjunction with a visiting nurse, a homemaker-home health aide assumes responsibility for the details of daily living for the homebound. These aides are trained primarily for patient care, but may do other household chores. Health insurance or Medicare and Medicaid sometimes cover the cost of this type of service, but the coverage has limitations.

Physical and Occupational Therapy

In some areas, either through private practices or visiting nurse services, physical and occupational therapists will make house calls. They may provide actual therapy during these visits, but they can also offer valuable suggestions for physical changes within the home to make it easier for the elderly person to function on a daily basis. Medicare may reimburse for this type of care.

Chore Services

Because they lack the physical strength and stamina or perhaps because they lack the financial resources, some elderly homeowners are unable to handle basic repairs or general maintenance. They may need help to change screens or storm windows, mow the lawn, rake leaves, clean gutters, fix leaky plumbing, and such. Many communities offer partly or fully funded projects to meet such needs. Others may provide help for basic homemaking tasks like vacuuming carpets or doing spring cleaning.

Nutrition Services

Nutrition is a major concern for people of all ages, for it helps to determine many aspects of health. For the elderly, though, a poor diet can be especially harmful. It can aggravate existing physical or mental problems, or it can create new ones.

Home delivery systems, such as Meals on Wheels,

can help. Its volunteers deliver hot meals to the homes of elderly shut-ins. This service offers a side benefit as well, for the volunteer may be the homebound person's sole contact on a regular, daily basis. His visit may become a real source of joy and anticipation. In addition, the volunteers become an important link in the vital chain that guards the senior citizen's well-being and safety, for they report back to the sponsoring agency regarding the general condition of people on their route.

Escort and Transportation Services

Some elderly people become homebound simply because of fear. They are afraid to leave their homes by themselves. And often with reason. Their neighborhoods may have become scary places where violent crime is all too familiar. Or the problem may be infinitely more subtle, as reflected in Corey Ford's comments, originally published in 1949: "Staircases are steeper than they used to be," and "everything is farther than it used to be." As for revolving doors, he said, "I have to let a couple of openings go past me before I jump in, and by the time I get up enough nerve to jump out again, I'm right back in the street where I started."[4]

Humorous to read, yes, but not funny to those who often find themselves threatened. Public stairways may be too steep, road signs may be hard to read, getting lost can be a threat to all. Thus many communities provide escort and transportation services specifically designed for elders.

Emergency Response Systems

Some hospitals, nursing homes, or other community-based agencies offer personal emergency services. The elder is given a "panic button," which she generally wears around her neck.

Let's suppose that Mrs. Smith has an emergency response system. When she presses the button, it transmits a signal to a machine attached to her home telephone. Automatically, the machine calls an operator at a designated homebase. The operator will call Mrs. Smith to determine the need and will respond appropriately. For instance, suppose Mrs. Smith, who has suffered for years from asthma, is experiencing difficulty breathing. The operator will call for emergency services. If Mrs. Smith doesn't answer her phone, the operator will send help immediately.

Negative reports have circulated regarding the reliability of some emergency response systems. I suggest that, as you evaluate the services available for you or your loved one, you should speak with each system's manager.

Find out where the system is located. Some will be outside your general area. Ask about the system's response time. Also ask about its liability coverages and about the interviewing procedure when the service calls to check on you or your loved one. And, finally, find out about the financial arrangements for payment.

The answers you gain by asking these questions will help you compare and evaluate the emergency response systems in your area. And don't forget that the Area Agency on Aging may be able to advise you on this decision.

Friendly Visiting

Some communities offer programs that enlist volunteers to visit the homebound. Participants stop by elders' homes on a regular schedule, and they simply spend time with those who cannot get out. They may participate in a hobby together, such as putting together jigsaw puzzles. They may work together to complete a minor chore. Or they may just sit and talk and share tea. They may do any number of things, but the important part of this service is that the elderly person receives a regular visit.

A similar resource involves a telephone-based service now available in some communities. Called a telephone reassurance system, the service enlists volunteers who will call senior citizens at a specified time each day to check on them. This service is especially valuable for senior citizens who live far away from their children. They may not need the emergency response system, but their children can't afford the long-distance charges involved in daily calls.

For additional information, you can contact the American Association of Retired Persons (AARP).

A Word About Hospice

Hospice may be one of the most widely recognized home health care organizations in the nation. It offers a special kind of care that provides sensitivity and support to people in the final stages of a terminal illness. The typical hospice patient has a life expectancy of six months or less. Hospice focuses on the unique needs of patients and their families, giving special attention to physical, emotional, social, and spiritual needs.

But hospice care is special because it emphasizes care over cure. It helps patients move to a level of comfort that allows them to live life fully as long as possible. The aim is to control pain consistently without damaging alertness. Services are provided by a team of trained professionals who offer medical care and personal support to the patient and his family.

Today, about 1,800 hospice programs are active in all fifty states. They serve about 200,000 families each year.

The National Hospice Organization is the only nonprofit organization devoted exclusively to hospice care. Initial funding comes from grants and contributions from charitable organizations as well as from local government funds and personal contributions. Beyond that, the organization receives money from local fundraisers, memorial gifts, voluntary contributions, and fees for patient services. Medicare, Medicaid, or private insurance carriers may pay those fees.

Some hospice programs offer free services for patients who do not qualify for reimbursement under any of those plans.

For additional information, call NHO's toll-free number at 1-800-658-8898, or write to the organization at 1901 N. Moore St., Suite 901, Arlington, VA 22209.

6

MOVING IN
WITH THE KIDS

My dad, as I've indicated, was a remarkable man. As I get older, I think I look more and more like him. I have two brothers, and the three of us were typical teenagers, putting him and my mother through their paces (and probably some misery).

Politically, Dad was more conservative than we youngsters were, and maybe we hurt him with some of our opinions, but I guess he was wise enough to know that sons do that to their fathers.

Anyway, by the time I was in my early twenties, that hurt had all melted away and we became friends. We grew even closer in later years.

Dad was widowed twice. In 1958 my mother, Edith, died. Two years later, Dad married Mary Louise, a widow who had been my mother's friend since their childhood. At Mary Louise's funeral in 1973, Dad simply told me, "It isn't any easier the second time."

It was a quiet, heart-stabbing remark that hit me with reality.

Though he was 74 years old by that time, my father lived alone in Ohio for a time after that. He frequently visited me in Arizona and my brothers in Texas and California. But he never had lived anywhere outside Ohio. He was hesitant to leave familiar surroundings, though we all invited him to live with us.

One harsh Ohio winter day, Dad climbed a tall ladder to install storm windows on a second-story casement. While he was in that uncomfortable position, I pointed out the advantages of Arizona weather.

"Why don't you come on out?" I suggested. "In Arizona, you don't do that—you don't have to put up storm windows. You don't even have to mow the lawn because you can just watch the cactus grow."

It Began with House-Sitting

Dad still didn't nibble at the bait, but eventually he agreed to house-sit for my wife, Ruth, and me while we took a trip outside the country. House-sitting reintroduced him to the benefits of the Arizona environment, and within a couple of years, he agreed to come and live with us.

As I mentioned earlier, he agreed to this move partly because he wasn't feeling well. The side effects of his blood pressure medication gave him symptoms that resembled Alzheimer's disease. He experienced mental lapses. A couple of times he had trouble finding his way home from downtown Phoenix.

Ruth insisted that he make an appointment with our physician, who set a major transformation in motion with changes in medication. Almost overnight, he looked and acted younger.

Dad lived with us for almost a decade after that. We had built a guest house in preparation for Ruth's mother to live with us. But in the end, she preferred to go to a nursing home, reluctant to leave Illinois and her other children. So Dad moved into the guest house.

Before he died in 1982, just a few months shy of his 84th birthday, he told us that his decade out West was the best ten years of his life. Naturally, he aged during that time, but in many ways he seemed to grow younger. He helped so much at my local office in Arizona and also with my wife's needlework company that eventually we convinced him to go on our payroll. His final years were happy and productive.

For all of us—my father and Ruth and me—living together was a positive experience. Ruth was completely supportive. She and I both had a terrific relationship with my father. And our home and living arrangements allowed all of us to be comfortable and to enjoy an appropriate measure of privacy. Our situation worked well because, in addition to fortunate financial undergirding, it was built on a foundation of good relationship and a blueprint of good planning.

Positives and Negatives

Admittedly, there are positive and negative aspects to this type of situation. On the plus side, intergenerational living provides a sense of continuity for family, especially for extended family and grandchildren; my father knew his great-grandchildren as teenagers. It may also provide companionship, particularly if you and your parent both have been living alone. It may offer peace of mind, not only regarding the quality of life for your parent but also regarding finances. If you choose to combine incomes, you may both enjoy greater financial freedom.

On the minus side, even though you are now an adult, you may be relegated to the child's role again, particularly if your parent tends to be aggressive or domineering. You may face the simple problems that come with more people in the same amount of space. The result may be increased work and decreased privacy.

You may have just seen your last child move out—now you're feeling this new responsibility at a time when you were expecting to be free. You may see the reemergence of old family stresses. Or your spouse and children may feel a need to compete for your attention.

For some people, the negatives will outweigh the positives. It is important to admit up front that this type of arrangement doesn't work for everyone. As one harried man told me, "We took Mom in to live with us.

You can't imagine the problems it caused. We weren't set up for it. We just couldn't do it."

And a woman talked about her relationship with her mother, who had moved in with her. "I can't tell you how difficult it is with two women in the house," she sighed, "especially two strong-willed women. Neither one of us knows where to draw the line, and she's just driving me crazy."

Exceptions Like Aunt Kate

Then there are those wonderful exceptions like my Aunt Kate, a woman with a fabulous attitude and outlook who chose not to move in with the children simply because she didn't want to burden the younger generation. Instead she went into a nursing home, where she was very happy and maintained a terrific sense of humor all of her days.

I remember going to see her in the nursing home one time, and I could hardly stop laughing; because of her character and personality, I knew she had made the right decision. At one point that day, she referred to a man down the hall from her. "His mind is shot," she said. "After all, he's over eighty." At that time, Aunt Kate was 82.

I've reflected on her great attitude and her choice to be independent in her own way, and I've wondered why some people are able to meet life head-on with a laugh, while others become so negative. I'm sure it has to do with an inner sense of security, but this self-confidence can be developed and is amenable to outside help.

Considering Living Together

Perhaps you are considering inviting your parent or elderly relative or friend to move in with you. Maybe your parent has gone far beyond the early warning signs listed in the previous chapter. Maybe your mother habitually forgets to turn off the stove, making you nervous about her safety. Maybe your father occasionally wanders away and can't find his way back home again. Or perhaps your aunt fell and broke her hip. Your mother and father may only need temporary care, but your aunt may need a long-term commitment.

Or maybe your dad is in the final stages of a serious illness, and he wants personal care in a family setting. You may be facing any of these or a vast number of other dilemmas.

If you are considering asking an elderly relative or friend to move in with you, please keep in mind that if your motivation is nothing more than a "sense of oughtness"—that is, if you are doing this only because you feel you should—your motivation may not be strong enough to support you for the long term.

Even if your motivations are completely pure, you must plan ahead. It's not enough to shrug your shoulders and assume that things will work out. It's not enough to surmise that you can rely on Sister Sue or Cousin Jane when the chips are down. It's not enough to expect that next-door neighbors will be happy to help.

You must take stock of the situation from all angles, and you must prepare for the future.

Define Your Relationship

If you have read this far in this book, the chances are pretty good that you are already a primary caregiver, or at least a prospective one. You probably already went through an evaluation process when you decided to assume that responsibility. Now, though, if you are seriously considering bringing your parent or elderly relative or friend into your home, I strongly suggest that you carefully evaluate every aspect of the situation.

Perhaps the best place to start is your relationship with the person who may move in with you. Define that relationship. I don't mean just in terms of mother-daughter or father-son, though that's an excellent place to start. But beyond that, determine your level of comfort with that relationship. You may even want to write down your feelings; writing will, of course, force you to put them into words.

Be realistic here. Don't succumb to hazy images of media ideals like Aunt Bee on "The Andy Griffith Show" and Uncle Charlie on "My Three Sons." Naturally, I don't want to demean the ideals, but we must face facts.

If your mother has been career-oriented all of her life, she probably is not going to turn into a sugar-coated, cookie-baking grandmother from a Norman Rockwell painting overnight—and maybe not ever.

If your father is used to running his own business, he may not be particularly interested in puttering around your garden, unless, of course, gardening has been one of his hobbies all along.[1]

In fact, consider this: If your parent is a corporate type used to hiring and firing, he may try to fire you as his caregiver. After all, any person who has always been aggressive may only grow more so if he feels his independence ebbing away.

Pondering these possibilities, it's good to remember that most of us—you and I, the caregivers—probably don't always exhibit the forbearance of Sheriff Andy Taylor.

Remember Unresolved Differences

As you realistically examine your relationship with the person who may move in with you, make sure you consider any unresolved differences from the past. How do they affect your feelings toward that person? Do you like him or her? Can you name three characteristics that you appreciate? Can you name three that annoy you? Which list was easier to create?[2]

And how have the two of you handled stress and conflict in the past? Has one been forceful and the other submissive? Has that pattern bred resentment? Have you both been argumentative? Are you ready now to handle that situation in your own home?

Already some of you are pausing a bit. Keep in mind, though, as you work through these issues, that past conflict doesn't necessarily cancel the possibility of living together. Angry words can't be erased, and hurt feelings may not heal right away. But past conflicts can be resolved, and future problems anticipated, if you all participate in frank and open discussion.

Living together always requires work, whether it involves a marriage or a parent-child relationship. Excess baggage from the past will only make it more difficult. As my friend Bob Butler explained, "Every family has its particular characteristics, and in some instances it would be hopeless and impossible for parents and children to live together." He added that this difficulty does not necessarily imply that "the children are cruel or insensitive. They may have had ample reason for feeling some resentment out of their own childhood and the way in which they were brought up and helped as children."

Of course, you may find that your elderly friend or relative doesn't want to move in with you. But you must take stock of your situation in case he or she agrees. In very simple words, the finest advice is this: Don't ask anyone if they want to move in with you unless you're ready for her or him to say yes.[3]

Your Personal Considerations

I also recommend you carefully evaluate yourself—your likes and dislikes, your place in this situation. How good are you at truly sympathizing with another person —at feeling what he or she feels? How well do you cope with stress? With change?

Do you have a good sense of humor? Can you legitimately characterize yourself as patient and flexible?

Also, examine your current situation. What are your present responsibilities? Which of these cannot be altered for any reason? Which are negotiable?

Is your life ordered in such a way that you can take on this additional responsibility? If not, is there any room for compromise?

Take stock of your own health. Do you have the physical and emotional stamina to provide the care that is needed?

And, finally, take a good look at your motivations. Why are you considering this type of living situation? And what good reasons do you have for rejecting this arrangement?

Physical Needs

Beyond defining your relationship and taking stock of personal considerations, you must determine your parent's physical and/or mental needs. You must practically evaluate your ability to meet them. What, if any, disabilities are involved? Realistically determine if those disabilities, and the care they require, are distasteful to you. Do you honestly believe you can learn to accept them?[4]

A call to your parent's physician or physical therapist is in order. Ask for specific information. How quickly does he or she expect that condition to decline? Please remember that the situation probably won't always be as it is now. Somewhere along the way, whether in the near future or many years away, your parent's condition will probably deteriorate. Begin now to plan a strategy to deal with that.

The Surroundings

Now that you have some understanding of your parent's physical and mental needs, it is important to take stock of your environment. Consider the assets and liabilities of your home.

Can you offer your parent his or her own room or living quarters? If not, what kind of compromise can you work out to ensure a measure of privacy for everyone involved?

What kind of physical alterations will be required to accommodate your parent's disabilities? As I mentioned in the previous chapter, some alterations may be fairly simple. You may simply need to place brightly colored tape at the edges of the stairs or in dark corners and to make sure the house is properly lighted, with no glare.

Those changes are simple and inexpensive. Some, though, will be more costly, in money and effort. For instance, you may need to:

- install wheelchair ramps,

- put grab-bars in the showers and bathtubs,

- install special toilets higher than normal.

It's wise to draw up a preliminary estimate of how much the necessary alterations will cost.

Involving Immediate Family

Include your immediate family in this evaluation process as well. In all likelihood, a change of this magnitude will affect them as well as you and your parent. I suggest that you call for a frank family discussion. Your spouse and children must understand what will be required of them.

Is everyone satisfied with the proposed arrangement? Why or why not? Can a compromise be reached to solve any or all of the "why nots"?

Does everyone agree to help fulfill the responsibility, both through moral support and through helping with the tasks required for care? Does everyone understand that, once the full range of responsibility is known, you will call another meeting to divide tasks according to the abilities of everyone?

And, even beyond the level of *understanding,* how does every family member *feel* about the scenario you present? Ask them to bring up *any* feelings they have.

What If You're Single?

Just in passing, I have a recommendation for those who are single and living alone. Don't feel pressured to work through this evaluation by yourself. You may want to talk this over with a friend, or even to make an appointment with a trained counselor or with a member of the clergy. He or she can help you come to grips with the questions I've suggested and perhaps can pinpoint some other issues you need to consider.[5]

Your Parents' Perspective

I heard recently of a couple who took a trip to visit their children. They were celebrating the husband's retirement. When they arrived at their youngest daughter's house, they were surprised to find that she and her husband had embarked on a major construction project. They were adding on to their house. You can imagine how their surprise multiplied when they learned that the extension was in process for their benefit. Without even asking, their daughter had assumed that, since they were retired, they would want to move in. In reality, this couple had already made other plans for the future.

Granted, this is an extreme case, but it should serve as a reminder that unless our parents are no longer mentally capable of making decisions we should not force them to comply with our desires. We can issue the invitation, but it is their choice to accept or reject. Keep in mind that a rejection today doesn't necessarily mean a rejection forever. As with my father, it may simply take some time to acclimate your parent or parents to the idea of moving in with you.

Perhaps the best rule of thumb for dealing with aging parents is one we learned as children—the Golden Rule. Treat your parents the way you want to be treated when you reach that age.

Out of respect, concentrate on helping them maintain their role in society. Don't do too much for them or overprotect them, so that they feel you are reducing them to the level of children. Respect their status as adults. And, again, let them make their own decisions as long as they are able to do so (and do so without trampling on the rights of others).

Involving Your Siblings

It is wise, in most cases, to try to involve your siblings in this evaluation. Again, chances are that you all went through this process when you selected a primary caregiver. But now, as demands increase, I recommend another family meeting to discuss the realities and perhaps to reassign responsibilities.

By this point in your evaluation, you should have a fairly good idea of your parent's needs. Outline them for your parent and your siblings. Ask for your parent's response, for in reality, despite your research, you may not have a handle on the issues your parent actually is facing.

Time to Make an Offer

Explain what you think you and your immediate family are prepared to offer, and ask for input. Don't be afraid to ask your relatives for help. Be honest about what you need and expect.

I would go so far as to suggest that you and your family draw up an informal written agreement outlining a plan for dividing the responsibilities of care. Your plan can be as specific as you want, but remember that each sibling's contribution will vary according to relationship, personal ability, and geographic nearness to your parents. Remember also that it is wise to plan for the possibility that care responsibilities will expand with time.

Discuss Finances and Legalities

In the midst of all this, make sure you discuss the financial and legal ramifications. Does your parent have the resources to help bear the costs of moving? Will any of your siblings help with the cost of care, not only in the present but in the future as well? Remember your list of alterations to your home; will anyone help you pay for those? All of these questions must go into the final decision.

Other Options

If you and your immediate family and your parent and siblings have worked through the process to this point and are still hesitant about making a final decision for the parent to move in with you, I suggest you explore other possibilities before acting.

If your parent has financial problems, he or she may want to look for a housemate to share expenses. Taking a roommate allows for companionship, and it provides a measure of personal security. The most common form of housesharing is offering to take in a "boarder." Serious students often make excellent matches for elders. Or your parent may wish to share a home with an old friend or someone she met at church or the senior center. References and addresses are important.

Of course, there may be disadvantages to such an arrangement. Personalities may clash. Or rent payments may increase your parent's income enough to affect Social Security, food stamps, or Medicaid. And zoning ordinances may limit the number of unrelated people who can share a single residential building.

Still, this option may be a viable consideration.

Shared-Group Residences

Sometimes you may find that nonprofit organizations in your area or in your parent's area can help you solve the matter. A few of them are buying or leasing homes or other buildings that can be remodeled. They convert those buildings into shared-group residences. Generally, each participant has a private bedroom, but bathrooms, living and dining rooms, kitchens, and laundry facilities are common areas.

Retirement Communities

In addition to these options, your parent may wish to check out retirement communities. Or you all may want to consider continuing-care communities. Most require newcomers to be at least 62 years old and to be able to live independently. Cottages or apartments are available for those who still are able to function on their own, but generally this type of community offers a nursing home or infirmary for those who need long-term care. Some also offer intermediate care, such as help with bathing and dressing.

Typically, this type of facility requires residents to pay a sizable fee up front. This is designed to cover the probable cost of eventual long-term care. Then monthly fees cover the ongoing cost of meals and other services.

Congregate Care

Another possibility is a congregate-care facility, designed specifically for those who are not quite able to function independently but who are not frail or feeble enough to require nursing home care. This type of facility generally offers your parent or elderly loved one a private apartment, usually equipped with a small kitchen suitable for fixing snacks. Meals, though, are served in a group dining area.

This type of program may also offer housecleaning services, fresh linens, planned recreation, and possibly even intermediate care, but it rarely includes nursing units suitable for long-term medical care.

Within the context of this book, I can provide only limited information about these resources. If you or your parent is interested in further information about any of these options, I suggest that you continue your research by calling the Area Agency on Aging in your locality or in the locality where your parent lives. Another source of information is the American Association of Retired Persons (AARP), headquartered in Washington, DC.

Perhaps a Counselor

It could be that none of these options suits your situation. If you have been through the evaluation process and have not found suitable rewards to encourage living together but have found no suitable alternatives, let me offer a word of caution. If you still feel obligated to assume care within your own home for your parent or elder relative, I suggest you and your family seek help from a trained counselor, perhaps the clergy of your church, to work through the process of adjusting to one another.

When It's Time to Begin

Should the decision be made that the parent will move in with you, it will be beneficial to call another meeting of your immediate family. Perhaps you will want to include the person who is moving in.

This is the time to establish guidelines for the changing relationship. Through open discussion, for instance, you may find that your parent is afraid you will take him for granted as a built-in baby-sitter. The family should resolve such issues before your parent moves in. And you should establish guidelines regarding the parent's involvement in disciplining your children. How much authority does he or she have?

You may want to discuss how much time you will spend together. You all will need a break.

If you and your spouse both work, how will your relative spend the day? Will he or she have any responsibilities for maintaining the household? And how do those responsibilities fit with the responsibilities assumed by you, your spouse, and your children?

Another area of concern is meal preparation. Preparing meals for someone on a special diet can be demanding.

It is important to prepare for intergenerational conflict as well. This may result from your father's lack of appreciation for your son's taste in music or for the volume at which he plays it. It may result from your mother's concern regarding your daughter's taste in fashion. Or it may result when Granddad eats the last chocolate chip cookie.

You can't avoid all conflict, but you would be wise

to set guidelines and to determine early how you will handle conflict when it arises.

Getting Ready for the Move

Once you and your immediate family have met and drawn up a plan of action, it is time to start working on any physical changes necessary to prepare your home. Begin to make your living quarters accident proof. We have already discussed some of the more obvious possibilities like wheelchairs and grab rails. Here is a checklist of other items to reckon with:

- Stairways, hallways, and pathways should be well lighted and free of clutter.

- Tightly fastened handrails should run the entire length of your stairs on both sides.

- Carpets should be firmly attached to the floors.

- Slick floors should have some type of rough-textured covering or abrasive strips to secure footing.

- Bathrooms should have nonskid mats or abrasive covering on any surface that might get wet.

- Each bathroom should have a night-light and, if your parent desires it, so should his room.

- A telephone, with perhaps a separate line, should be installed in your parent's living quarters.

- A private thermostat or additional heaters should be located in the parent's quarters.

For more suggestions of fairly inexpensive ways to prepare your home, you can write to the U.S. Consumer Product Safety Commission, Washington, DC 20207. Through this commission, you can obtain a free copy of a booklet titled *Home Safety Checklist for Older Consumers*.

In Case of Dementia

Also, if the person moving in is suffering from dementia or another mental disability, brainstorm with your family for creative ways to make your home familiar and secure. This is especially important for those who might be prone to wandering.

Beyond the practicalities of accident prevention and security, consider ways to make your parent feel welcome in your home. Perhaps you can redecorate his bedroom using his own furniture. Or you may consider putting your father's favorite recliner in your living room, or using your mother's dishes. Regardless of careful planning, your father or mother will probably feel displaced at first, and these simple measures will help your parent adjust.

Moving Day

It is important to remember that moving day will be stressful for you and your family and for the person moving in. If possible, have the house, or at least the bedroom where your parent will stay, ready before she arrives. Don't be surprised if, despite your best efforts, your parent feels like a burden. If she has to observe all of the changes being made for her accommodation, that feeling may intensify.

Don't treat this day as a commonplace occurrence. Everyone involved is experiencing changes that will impact each individual and each relationship. It may be necessary to discuss together any feelings of anxiety or uncertainty.[5]

The Long-Term Situation

Various factors in your relationship and living conditions may change with time. Keep lines of communication open with your spouse, with your children, and with your parent. Honest discussion and flexibility from all parties should solve most of the problems that you face in the long term.

Dealing with Stress

Regardless of how well you have planned, you probably will experience times of stress with the arrangement. It may come from the outside, through criticism from family members who, despite their nit-picking, are unwilling to help. It may come from the inside, in your attempt to maintain your relationships with your spouse and children in the midst of increasing responsibility. This is especially true for the "sandwich generation"—adults who are caught between caring for parents and children at the same time.

The pressure may come from any number of sources, but regardless of why stress comes, it is important to realize that it *will* come. And increased stress, with no opportunity for relief, raises the chance for burnout.

According to some studies, for most caregivers, financial concerns cause less stress than the emotional pressures of this kind of situation. This is especially true for those persons caring for elders with mental disabilities. This fact becomes increasingly important with the growing number of people who are victims of Alzheimer's disease or other forms of dementia. Families providing care for Alzheimer's patients report three times more stress symptoms than the general population. I will discuss the particular problems of Alzheimer's disease in Chapter 8.

Symptoms of the Pressure

Symptoms that typically accompany this type of pressure include depression, anger, anxiety, frustration, guilt, sleeplessness, demoralization, helplessness, irritability, and emotional exhaustion. Related considerations include restrictions to time and freedom, isolation from friends and social activities; difficulty in setting priorities; and perhaps a disruption of the caregiver's career.[6]

The burdens of caregiving are interrelated. In addition to the emotional burdens, caregiving can take an enormous toll on a person's physical health and stamina —especially for a small person who is caring for a larger person.

As one expert put it, "Caregivers are the invisible laborers without whom neither the health care system nor the frail elderly could survive."[7] Yet their invisibility may exclude them from the benefit of programs that will care for *their* needs. In short, caregivers need an opportunity to rest.

Respite Care

Because of a growing understanding of this need, many localities are now offering *respite care* for caregivers. Respite can be defined as an interval of temporary relief, but because the needs of the caregivers are so varied, there is no real guarantee as to what services will be included in respite care. Beyond the central purpose of providing rest for caregivers, there are many variations.

You may find in your situation that your friends and family members will help you out. They may come to your home and stay with your parent or elderly loved one to enable you to take a break. But if you don't have that kind of help, or if you simply need more of it, check into the possibilities for respite care in your community.

One avenue, which we will cover in the next chapter, is adult day care. But it is not your only option. Respite care services incorporate the combined resources of community hospitals, social-service agencies, day-care centers, and nursing homes. They may even offer the services of a health worker who will come to your home to provide some relief in caring for your parent or elderly friend.

Don't be afraid to admit that you need some rest and to seek out help. If you have the opportunity to take a break—perhaps even to go away for a couple of weeks —you will find it easier to resume your responsibilities when you return. And because this type of care is so necessary, more and more insurance companies are agreeing to cover the cost.

If you want more information about respite care services in your area, contact your local Area Agency on Aging, your senior center, your local social services, and any support groups available for those caring for senior citizens. Your own health—physical, emotional, and mental—is a precious commodity. Don't take it for granted.

7

HOME AWAY
FROM HOME

Meet Margaret Patrick and Ruth Eisenberg. Both women were partly paralyzed by strokes in 1982. For Mrs. Patrick, a black woman in her senior years, the stroke affected her right side. For Mrs. Eisenberg, a Jewish woman also a senior, the stroke affected her left side.

The two women met at an innovative senior day-care center in New York's Westchester County, where they discovered their shared love of the piano. It was to be the making of a classic piano duo known as Ebony and Ivory. Mrs. Patrick played bass with her left hand, and Mrs. Eisenberg played treble with her right. Their lives took on new meaning.

Adult day care transformed the lives of Mrs. Patrick and Mrs. Eisenberg. It restored to them a talent and an emotional outlet they thought they had lost forever. It renewed their sense of purpose and gave them a safe place to be involved in the lives of other people. They discovered a firm foundation on which to build a relationship.

But Mrs. Patrick and Mrs. Eisenberg are not alone. They serve as a symbol that these programs really work. Day care is bringing out this type of energy and vitality in a high percentage of the more than 100,000 senior citizens and developmentally disabled individuals participating in adult day care all across America.

Many authorities are now recognizing this service as a valuable resource in the full slate of care options. I am willing to go a step further. I believe adult day care is one of the most exciting and innovative resources available today for elders and their families.

The Value of Day Care

One important reason for my confidence in the value of such programs is that adult day care meets caregiving needs at many levels.

It can extend the time that seniors live independently, for example. In fact, according to a 1985-86 survey of day-care participants, those living independently make up the second largest subgroup utilizing this resource. The survey concluded that, for many of these seniors, adult day care is the primary factor that is making continued independence a viable option.[1]

In addition, adult day care is a precious resource for family members and friends who are providing various levels of care. Caregivers are at risk. Their responsibility has the potential to drain them of emotional and physical reserves. Regardless of whether your parent or elderly friend actually lives with you or is managing to live fairly well on his own, caregiving is a huge task. Adult day care provides the opportunity for the caregiver to lead a fairly normal life—normal, of course, in the sense that you can participate in at least some of the activities you enjoyed before you took on this additional responsibility.

Your Work Schedule Can Go On

Day care may allow caregivers to continue working their regular, daily schedule. As Val Halmandaris of the National Association for Home Care said, "Adult day care is a wonderful option. More and more, as both husband and wife within a family work, there is a need to have someone look after an aged relative. When there is concern that Uncle Louie might set the house on fire, how much better it is to have the option of taking him to a day-care facility where he can have a meal, perhaps take a nap, have some instruction, have an opportunity to engage in play, have an opportunity to exercise. Day care is something that is very exciting, not only for young children but for the elderly of our nation as well."

Not Only for Children

Unfortunately, some people still struggle with the terminology used to define this service. As Betty Ransom of the National Institute on Adult Daycare, said, "A lot of people think of day care and they think of children. They think, 'That's not for my mom.' "[2] But maybe when you look at your options, you will find that it is for your mom.

Day Care Helps in Alzheimer's Case

In fact, in the opinion of one woman in Norfolk, Virginia, day care may be *exactly* what your loved one needs. Perhaps you remember Betty Ritter, whom I referred to in Chapter 4. She has been caring for her husband, a victim of Alzheimer's disease, for fourteen years. Betty believes adult day care is the one thing that has kept her husband from giving in to the onslaught of the disease.

"It has kept him stimulated," she said. "It's something he looks forward to." And, she added, "I almost feel as if day care is more important for an older person than for a child. The stimulation keeps him in the community."

Mrs. Ritter believes some people resist putting loved ones in adult day care because they feel they are deserting them. "When I first started looking into this, I cried," she acknowledged. "I felt like I was turning him over to someone else." But, she said, the advantages have been incredible for her and for her husband. "I just can't say enough about day care."

Day Care Provides Rest

In addition to helping you keep up with your career, adult day care may also provide a much-needed rest from the rigors of responsibility. The same 1985-86 survey I noted before found that the largest subgroup of participants using this service were elderly people living with a spouse or another relative or friend. The report explained that, because it offered respite to caregivers, day care might be the primary "enabling factor" keeping many of these people in the community rather than confined to an institution.[3]

Emotional Reassurance

Day care may also provide emotional reassurance. For some caregivers and their families, the health and safety of their elderly loved one becomes a constant source of worry. A day-care facility can provide great comfort, simply through the assurance that your parent or friend is getting quality supervision.

A Historical Perspective

Because the public is coming to understand the many advantages of this resource, the concept is growing rapidly in America. But this growth has been a long time coming.

The basis for adult day care actually rests in the 1940s, in psychiatric day hospitals where the primary function was to help patients after they were released from mental institutions. In the 1950s, though, a geriatric day hospital program began in England. Its purpose was to accelerate the possible return of hospitalized, aging patients to their own homes.

By the 1960s, this program had inspired interest in the United States. And the day care concept here shifted its focus. No longer was day care limited to those with psychiatric needs, but it began to take on other health maintenance. Centers began to operate independently in Arizona, Pennsylvania, and Minnesota.[4]

In the decade of the 1970s, adult day care programs spread as a grassroots effort to meet a real need in society. Prompted by negative reports about long-term institutional care, concerned citizens continued to build on the established foundation. Influenced heavily by the holistic emphasis characterizing that decade, adult centers united health care and social services within a relaxed setting. The goal was to help those who were not quite able to function independently.[5]

A Surge in the 1980s

Nationally, adult day care's growth was slow for a while. But in the 1980s, fueled mainly by the efforts of the National Institute on Adult Daycare, founded in 1979 through the National Council on Aging (NCOA), this concept took off.

In 1978, an official federal directory listed only 300 adult day-care centers operating in only 40 states and serving about 5,000 people. By 1989, just over a decade later, the numbers had swelled to more than 2,000 centers operating in all 50 states and serving more than 70,000 people.[6]

And still they spread. In 1993, according to the National Institute on Adult Daycare, the United States has about 3,000 centers serving more than 102,000 people.

The Current Situation

Given these statistics, you can see that no matter where you are in the United States, you can probably find a day-care center in or reasonably near your area or in the area where your parent or elderly friend is living. Perhaps the best place to begin your search is with the Area Agency on Aging in that locality. You may also want to consult your local social services or health department, mental health centers, community centers, or senior centers. Your physician possibly can advise you, or you can call the Eldercare Locator.

But once you find a center or perhaps even a variety of centers from which to choose, what will it look like? Well, according to statistics provided by the National Institute on Adult Daycare, we know that a typical facility averages 34 to 35 participants per week, and the average daily cost is less than $40. That's a fraction of the cost of institutional care or private nursing.

And Medicaid may help to cover the costs in some situations and in some states. But, of course, there is considerable variance in the fees, from facility to facility, just as there is in every facet of adult day care.

The Similarities

In spite of widespread national development, this resource is still difficult to capsulize. The services offered vary from community to community, even from center to center; therefore, it is hard to describe adult day care in a nutshell.

All adult programs do share a common philosophy, which rests on three key points. First, according to a position paper established by the National Institute on Adult Daycare, these programs salute the individuality of participants and recognize their strengths, weaknesses, and potential for growth.

Second, they have a holistic view of the needs of participants. They recognize an interrelationship among the physical, social, emotional, and environmental aspects of real well-being.

Third, they seek to create an environment that will encourage a positive self-image among participants. This is vital for "restoring, maintaining, and stimulating capacities for independence while providing supports for functional limitations."

The position paper also notes that all participants in adult day care are somehow limited in their ability to function in complete independence. "Peer interaction," it concludes, "stimulates conversation and the motivation to strive for greater independence."[7]

The Differences

Given this philosophical background, let me take a stab at describing the kinds of facilities you may find in your community.

Traditionally, adult day-care programs have fallen into two categories. Some, often sponsored by or housed in a hospital or nursing home, are considered "medically based." Others, often provided by churches or other community organizations, are considered "socially or recreationally based."

The Medically Based Facility

In medically based facilities, nurses may provide supervision and counseling for medical problems. They may maintain communication with the participant's family and personal physician regarding sudden health changes. They may even recommend changes in medications.

These facilities also may offer therapy services, which can be a tremendous relief to families who cannot afford the equipment necessary. And different types of therapy can address a variety of needs.

Occupational therapy, for example, provides physical, social, and emotional help designed to restore and maintain skills that enable a senior to care for himself. Speech therapy, especially valuable for stroke victims, helps to restore, improve, and maintain clear speech. And remotivation therapy helps participants to recover

139

emotionally from loss. This therapy addresses not only the loss of a loved one; it may also include the loss of personal independence or security through illness or injury.

The Social/Recreational Based Facility

Community based facilities, on the other hand, generally fall into the second category. They have nurses, aides, and other professionals on staff for general supervision, but they may not offer services like rehabilitation. They probably do provide daily blood pressure checks and other procedures to track the general health of their participants. According to traditional wisdom, though, these centers exist primarily to meet the social and recreational needs of participants.

These categories are nice for description and definition, but some experts indicate they may be "arbitrary and even misleading."[8] Most centers cross over the boundaries, so the facilities in your community probably will offer a variety of services from each type of adult day care.

Most programs, for example, in addition to providing general medical supervision and care, help to meet participants' basic physical needs. They may promote group exercise, or at least sitting exercises that can include anyone who cannot walk or stand for long periods.

Many centers also provide a hot meal each day, or at least meal supplements, depending on the nutritional needs of those involved. And some centers even provide special times for visiting hairstylists, barbers, or possibly manicurists to pamper the participants.

Beyond addressing these necessities of life for the elderly, most adult day centers, regardless of which category they may fall into, provide activities designed to meet seniors' social and recreational needs. For instance, they may furnish educational programs that encourage learning. One of the nasty lies that plagues our society is "You can't teach an old dog new tricks." I'm not in a position to debate the literal meaning of this proverb—it might be true about dogs. But I can guarantee that it isn't true about people. You can teach new information to older people, and adult day care provides a forum that makes such learning possible.

Centers may also offer cultural activities, such as movies, plays, choral performances, dance recitals, and special speakers. And they may offer recreational opportunities such as board games or tournaments or daily craft projects. One center in Rockville, Maryland, invited a former member of a dance company to entertain. But she did more than just perform—she enlisted participants to join her. She asked them to dance.[9]

The Benefits

The positive aspects of these programs are numerous. Some benefits, such as monitoring health conditions and providing rehabilitation services, are self-evident. Others, though, are hidden much more deeply, lying at the level of emotional need.

Adult day care offers a support system for those who feel inadequate to face the jarring reality of a changing world. The relationships cultivated within this environment remind people that they're not alone with their problems or their fears. They help the elderly to focus on the future rather than anchor their sense of reality in the past.

And what is the result? For many participants, adult day-care programs offer a structured environment that allows them to find social stimulation and renewed self-esteem.

Lois Oliver, director of a center in Wisconsin, explained it this way: "We have children bringing in their mother and saying, 'She can't do this anymore, she can't do that.' Within a day or two she'll be in the kitchen making muffins and feeling good about herself."[10]

A Specific Example

So what exactly does adult day care look like? Maybe you can get a better feel for this type of program if I actually take you to a day-care facility in Norfolk, Virginia. Called the Adult Day-Health Care Centers, this program has been serving the public since 1975. It is fully licensed and operated by the Commonwealth of Virginia.

The entire program is actually housed in two locations. One facility is within the senior center itself. Jill Ecklesdafer, supervisor at this particular site, said this location provides a unique opportunity for frail seniors in the day-care center to relate to seniors who are more active. The other facility is situated at Norfolk's Jewish Community Center. Although most of the participants are not Jewish, this center observes Jewish traditions and serves Kosher food.

A coordinator oversees the workings of both facilities. Ecklesdafer, as I said, works out of the senior center. Other staff members at this site include a nurse, an activity coordinator and assistant, and a senior companion.

The staff of this center is planning for growth, so it is licensed for thirty-nine participants, based on its square footage. But it currently averages ten to fifteen participants a day. The staff provides general medical supervision and dialogues with the participant's family or physician if they notice any changes.

The facility itself is spacious and bright. At one end of the main room, participants might be playing Po-Ke-No or Bingo at the pair of tables set up specifically for such activity. You can tell from their conversation that the participants have developed friendships with one another. They are gregarious, and they help one another naturally.

A spinet piano leans against one wall, perhaps resting from the load of hymnals and 1940s music that announces the tastes of the in-house musicians.

At the other end of the airy room, easy chairs and sofas create a living-room atmosphere, complete with a stereo and television. A participant named Virginia is sitting in an orange overstuffed chair singing, "I'm Looking Over a Four-Leaf Clover."

She stops long enough to mention that she is 75 years old. "Most people don't think I look that old," she smiles, pushing back her white hair with a dark finger. She strokes her purple skirt as she adds that her favorite activity at the center is the daily exercise period. "It's good for your health," she says. "It keeps your bones limber."

Exercise is an integral part of the center's daily schedule, but Ecklesdafer admits to some difficulty in planning activities. The staff also plans various arts and crafts projects for the participants. They enjoy these activities, but also, the staff knows they improve the strength and flexibility of their hands and fingers. "It's challenging," Ecklesdafer said, "because we handle a variety of disabilities. One participant might be blind, another deaf, and another confined to a wheelchair."

She added that stroke victims are wonderful candidates for day care. Two side effects commonly afflict stroke victims. The first is depression, and the second is isolation brought on by decreased mobility. Some stroke patients begin to lose hope. "If all of a sudden you feel like you *can't* do anything, you probably *won't* do anything anymore," she explained.

Day care puts these participants in a relaxed atmosphere where they are encouraged to enjoy exercise and other activities that can increase their mobility. In addition, it offers stroke victims the opportunity to build relationships with others who are facing similar challenges. They can encourage one another.

Alzheimer's patients also can benefit greatly from day care, particularly in the early stages of the disease. Ecklesdafer noted that the center where she works is not really equipped to handle these patients "once they reach the point of compulsive wandering." Some facilities, though, are specifically designed to meet the needs of Alzheimer's victims and their families.

A Variety of Demands

As you can see, adult day care centers do meet a variety of needs. How can one facility respond to so many demands? One key is a daily schedule that offers a diversity of activities.

A typical day at the Adult Day-Health Care Center begins at 9:30 A.M. with "Moments for Expression." Designed to be mentally stimulating, this time may be used to involve participants in a discussion of current events. Or perhaps the staff will simply invite participants to reminisce.

This session is followed by a forty-five-minute coffee break, and then a period of "Sittercise," which features sitting exercises designed to keep seniors moving. "A lot of people come in with their parents," Ecklesdafer said with a smile, "and they say, 'Just get them to do *something*. All they do is sit and watch TV.' "

So the program includes this daily exercise time, not only for the participants' physical health but also to "keep them moving."

Activities vary in the next hour. One day the center may offer pet therapy. Another day it might sponsor board games or "table volleyball," or perhaps even "Name That Tune."

Lunch is delivered in time for participants to eat at 12:30.

The afternoon offers a mixed bag of social and recreational activities, which may be theme-oriented. On Valentine's Day, for instance, the staff may plan craft projects that emphasize a sweetheart theme.

Children and Seniors

One exciting new program at the Adult Day-Health Care Center allows seniors to enjoy activities with "adopted grandkids" from a nearby children's day-care center. "Most children don't seem to be reluctant," Ecklesdafer said. "And we try to create an environment which allows for informal, personal contact."

Actually, this is part of a relatively new concept called "intergenerational day care," which is opening new opportunities to bridge generation gaps.

Ina Koenig, director of an adult day-care center in Pompano Beach, Florida, said her seniors meet once a month with local preschoolers for special activities. "It's an unwritten love agreement," she said. "The little ones—their parents have to work, so they're not there to give them warmth. The seniors are in the same situation, so we bring them together to fulfill the needs of both."[11]

Very little data exist to comment on the value of bringing children and seniors together. Still, some experts have noticed a special bond between children and elders.

Pat Moore, for instance, is a young woman who disguised herself as an old woman for three years, from 1979 to 1981. When she started her masquerade, she was only 26, but her disguise was designed to make her look 80 to 85 years old. Dressed in her costume, she visited 116 cities in fourteen states and two Canadian provinces and recorded her observations in a book titled *Disguised.*

After noting various reactions from people of different age and socioeconomic groups, Moore described a chance meeting with a 6-year-old boy on a beach in Florida. He invited her to join him in feeding the gulls and then took her on a walk to collect shells. When they parted, he kissed her cheek and waved good-bye as he galloped down the shoreline to return to his grandmother's house for dinner.

"For my six-year-old friend," Moore wrote, "there was no young or old, no victims or stereotypes, no barriers of age at all. There was just friendship, and laughter, and a big wonderful beach with plenty of shells for two friends to share."

Later she added, "Why can young children usually be counted on to offer such acceptance? Because they have not yet learned that elderly people are 'different' in any critical way."[12]

Intergenerational Opportunities

Some day-care centers are capitalizing on this openness between children and seniors. One center in Burlington, Vermont, involves seniors and children ages 2 to 5 in intergenerational gardening.

Another center, in Union, New Jersey, is extending the concept to include high school students. In fact, the center set up housekeeping on the campus of a local high school. The new location is great, according to the coordinator, because it provides facilities for the seniors to enjoy art, music, and physical fitness opportunities. In addition, the participants can visit the high school's vocational department. They can go to the cosmetology classes to have their hair styled or to enjoy a manicure. The program also offers a wonderful opportunity to introduce high school students to job possibilities in allied health services.[13]

Nationally, about 10 percent of adult day-care centers are considered to be intergenerational facilities. That means they serve both age groups simultaneously. Schedules feature separate activities as well as joint activities for children and seniors.

Corporate Success Story

Stride Rite Corporation, a shoe manufacturer head-quartered in Cambridge, Massachusetts, has taken the concept of intergenerational day care to a new level. The corporation, recognized as a pioneer in family-oriented employee benefits, opened one of the nation's first corporate day-care centers for children in 1971. In 1990, the center opened its doors to seven new participants, all elderly, and it became a true intergenerational facility.

The program was deemed successful by young and old. A 5-year-old participant told a national news magazine, "I like doing things with the ladies."

A 71-year-old participant noted, "The children give us life."[14]

That, after all, is what it's about.

8

FACTS AND MYTHS
OF DEMENTIA

O ne very nasty rumor that regularly circulates
in our society says old people are destined for
senility. And the term *senility* has become a derogatory
catchword that lumps all kinds of forgetfulness. In lay
usage it is merely a term of abuse. The medical use of
the word is restricted and concise.

Unhappily, its misapplication to the elderly has its
root in a long history of Western age discrimination.

Samuel Johnson, the noted eighteenth-century English writer, critic, and lexicographer, spoke of it this
way: "There is a wicked inclination in most people to
suppose an old man decayed in his intellect. If a young
or middle-aged man, when leaving a company, does
not recollect where he laid his hat, it is nothing; but if
the same inattention is discovered in an old man, people
will shrug their shoulders and say, 'His memory is going.' "[1]

When we take time to examine the facts, though,

we will find a very different picture of senility among our elders from what rumor claims.

Just the Facts

The fact is that the term *dementia* takes in a variety of symptoms that arise from diseases or disorders that damage the brain, causing people to experience a progressive loss of brain function. Alzheimer's disease, which accounts for about half the cases of dementia, has received the most publicity, but other causes include Pick's disease, Creutzfeldt-Jakob disease, Huntington's disease, Parkinson's disease, and various unclassified dementias.

About 30 percent of the population will eventually develop some form of dementia, if they live long enough. But among the over-65 crowd, only about 6 percent suffer from Alzheimer's. Unfortunately, that percentage rises to 47.2 percent in those age 85 and older.[2]

A Description of Dementia

Dementia itself is widely misunderstood, even by many in the medical profession. Dementia is not a disease, but a label assigned to a group of symptoms that result from certain diseases and conditions. And those symptoms seem to follow the same course generally.

Diseases causing dementia affect the brain, causing a disorder that brings about a steady but gradual, slow deterioration of the brain's functions. On the average, this deterioration may last seven to nine years, at which point the patient dies. There are recorded cases, however, of people who have endured such diseases for twenty or more years.[3]

The first noticeable symptoms of dementia generally involve memory lapses. Of course, occasional memory lapses are normal. The fact that you occasionally, or even regularly, misplace your car keys does not necessarily mean you have Alzheimer's disease. It may mean absolutely nothing. Or it may mean that you are suffering from other problems, including depression or stress, or that you are taking certain medications with side effects that mimic the symptoms of dementia. Dr. Roy Menninger put misplacing car keys in perspective: "If you forget where you put your car keys, it is probably not Alzheimer's. If you forget what your car keys are for, then you have a problem."

But continual and irreversible memory lapses may be warning signs, particularly if they affect areas of life that are habitual for the individual involved. For instance, dementia may suddenly render an accountant incapable of adding a column of figures.[4] That phenomenon is a warning sign.

In the first stages of dementia, short-term memory often is affected while long-term memory may still be very accurate. But beyond the loss of short-term memory, the individual who suffers from dementia may experience a loss of logical and social ability. He may be able to continue performing established routines, but he may lose the ability to process new information and to adapt to new situations.

Dementia sufferers also tend to be unable to deal with abstracts. They may have difficulty, for instance, prioritizing a list of tasks.

Eventually, the dementia victim will experience changes in his ability to process language, in his general thought processes, in his personality, and in his body. He may even lose the ability to recognize family members.

People who were quite docile before the onset of the disease may become temperamental and angry. But uncharacteristic fits of emotion or hypersexuality eventually will erode to apathy.

Eventually, the victim may experience changes in nervous control of muscles. This will result in rigidity and cramping, perhaps even seizures, in addition to the inability to chew and swallow. In time, she will become bedridden and incontinent, finally losing consciousness and eventually dying, often because of a secondary illness.

Secondary Dementia

Perhaps the preceding description has frightened you, for indeed, Alzheimer's disease and the other conditions that cause dementia are frightening ailments. But keep in mind that the symptoms of dementia actually can result from factors that don't affect the brain directly. These conditions can cause *secondary dementia*.

The factors causing secondary dementia may include a number of diseases, along with malnutrition and exposure to certain drugs or toxins. On account of such factors, there are documented cases of misdiagnosis of dementia. Some authorities contend that almost one-third of patients who suffer from dementia-like symptoms actually have fully treatable conditions.[5]

For instance, *depression* is a common cause of secondary dementia. Common physical symptoms of depression include headache and/or dizziness and fainting, blurred vision, rapid heartbeat, loss of bodily control resulting in the dropping of things or falling, breathing difficulty, heartburn and nausea, along with stomach spasms and chest pains, pressure in the bladder, cramps, sweating, and even itching or tingling in the skin.

Beyond that, depression can mirror dementia so closely that diagnosis can be truly difficult. The distinction is made even more difficult by the fact that many dementia victims actually suffer from depression, particularly in the early stages of the disease when they are aware that things aren't quite right. In addition, medications prescribed for depression may cause some problems with intellectual functions, and those problems can easily be regarded as dementia.

Vascular disease, traditionally known as hardening of the arteries, is another common cause of secondary dementia. This type of disease limits the supply of blood and its nutrients to the brain, impacting the brain's ability to function. Vascular disease is treatable, as are other problems that may induce symptoms of dementia.

Chronic infections, such as bronchitis and pneumonia, may also be culprits. Older people are more likely to develop chronic smoldering infections. The term refers to infection that progresses through the patient's system without producing the obvious symptoms typically related to the illness. These infections can produce symptoms that mirror dementia. But discovery and treatment of the infection's source can bring dramatic results.

Other possible causes of secondary dementia are alcoholism, side effects of medications, hydrocephalus (water on the brain), hormonal imbalances, and malnutrition.

Diagnosis of Alzheimer's and Related Disorders

At present, the only method available to diagnose Alzheimer's disease and related disorders with certitude is examination of brain tissue. Microscopic examination at an autopsy will show that a brain affected by Alzheimer's disease, for instance, plays host to tangles of fibers and clusters of degenerating nerve endings in areas of the brain that control memory and intellectual functions.

Most victims, however, are diagnosed through a battery of psychological, physical, and neurological tests designed to rule out other possibilities.

Formal psychological tests provide confirmation of

deficits in memory. The questions test the patient's ability to recall simple facts, but they also allow the psychiatrist or psychologist to evaluate any possible deterioration in the patient's language skills in formulating the answers.

In the case of an individual exhibiting symptoms like dementia, a thorough examination should include a detailed medical history, neuropsychological testing, blood work, urinalysis, chest X-ray, and electrocardiogram (EKG). These tests enable the doctor to check for heart disease, circulatory difficulties, diabetes, and other disorders.

Beyond that battery of common physical tests, a doctor probably will require an electroencephalogram (EEG), which records voltage patterns from the brain. A cerebrospinal fluid examination is another possibility. Both tests are relatively easy. Neither can provide a positive diagnosis of Alzheimer's, but they can rule out other possibilities.

Head X-rays are of little value in this process, since they cannot produce an image of the brain. But CAT scans are another story. The CAT scan can outline the brain in "slices," so the specialist can view it at several levels. This imaging can help in the diagnosis of strokes, for instance—even minor ones. But again, it cannot necessarily detect the cause of dementia.[6]

According to the Alzheimer's Association, this kind of detailed examination ensures that the accuracy of diagnosis is about 90 percent.[7]

In the course of all this testing and examination, it is

important to keep in mind that the patient or his family *always* has the right to seek a second opinion. You can ask your doctor or specialist to recommend someone, or you can choose another doctor yourself.

Research

At this time, no cure has been discovered for the diseases that cause dementia. However, recent findings offer hope. Research concentrates on searching for a cause, a better method of diagnosis, and a cure. Until scientists are successful in those areas, experiments with treatment continue.

Most drugs being used to combat Alzheimer's disease and related disorders attempt to treat the cognitive or intellectual symptoms. Other treatments target behavioral problems.

Practical Concerns of Daily Life

About 65 percent of Alzheimer's and other dementia victims are cared for in the home. The increasing forgetfulness associated with these diseases may cause a number of problems in that situation. If you are a primary caregiver, for instance, you may be forced to restrict some of the patient's activities, such as driving a car. Unfortunately, the loss of ability to drive safely is often sensed by the caregiver before it is evident to the driver, and this can cause a feeling of insult and persecution that is not easy to deal with. Some patients will experience difficulty with numbers, so they may not be able to tell time or to count change. Some may wander and get lost.

Although there are no known cures for the diseases and disorders that cause dementia, there are ways to make life easier for the victims and their caregivers.

Basic Grooming

The dementia victim will eventually reach a stage where he or she will need help with basic grooming. Your father may forget how to shave, or your mother may forget how to apply makeup or style her hair. I suggest you ask a professional—perhaps your parent's barber or beautician—to teach you how to perform these tasks. These simple measures will help both you and the patient to feel better about his or her appearance.

Wardrobe is another issue. At first, labeling clothing will help the dementia victim to dress himself in clothes that match. Eventually, though, he probably will need additional help. You may need to lay out clothing for him, and eventually you may even need to stay with him to be sure he puts on the clothing in the right order. It's not unusual, for instance, for a dementia victim to put his underwear on over his clothing.

Mother Teresa's Unshakeable Focus

I've talked frequently about the value of attitude in lengthening active life in a world that tends to relegate seniors to the shelf on the basis of age alone. No one offers a better example of the point than Mother Teresa, who simply keeps going in her service of the destitute, the desperately sick, and the castaways, regardless of her own condition.

What a better world this would be were there more people with such strong motivation and attitude. Mother Teresa does not question for a moment her calling to serve others, and that is what she intends to do whether she's in her forties or her eighties. She believes God will keep her here as long as he desires, and she refuses to let painful health stop her.

She revealed her unshakeable focus when I met her in Los Angeles, where she was busy making the rounds in her work among the suffering. My daughter was with her and as they approached me, she said, "Mother Teresa, I want you to meet my father." Obviously wanting to please my daughter, she stopped, shook my hand, said hello, and unaffectedly asked, "And what line of work are you in?"

"I'm in television."

"That's nice," she said politely and continued with her work. Priorities like that will not be defeated.

Help at Mealtime

A dementia victim's loss of memory will eventually affect mealtime. I suggest you brainstorm and consider any options that may help the patient and the rest of the family avoid confusion during this time.

For instance, if every member of the family has an established chair at the table, and she sits in that chair at every meal, this will help the dementia victim feel more confident.

Also, consider any measures that will help to limit the patient's options at mealtime. You may avoid meals that involve passing several dishes at once. If possible, serve just one thing at a time. And limit the choices for silverware. Sometimes, for instance, you can plan meals that require only a spoon. Or if you serve sandwiches, cut them into small pieces so the dementia victim won't even have to use her knife.

When She Wanders

When the victim reaches the wandering stage, it may be wise to secure your home with new or additional locks. This may be especially important if the patient tends to wander at night, when the caregiver is asleep.

You may want to have her wear an identification bracelet and a Medic-Alert bracelet.

Consider structuring her environment in a way that

will help her avoid getting lost. You may find this necessary even in her own home. For example, you may want to push her bed against the wall so she can get out only on one side. This will avoid confusion by limiting options. For instance, it will automatically get her started in the right direction if she has to use the bathroom at night.

Of course, you will want to do everything possible to accident proof the home where she is living. In addition to taking measures that inhibit falling, you should put chemical cleansers and other toxins where they can't be reached. You also may want to put away electrical appliances, medications, fragile knickknacks, and valuables.

Dealing with Insomnia

In the course of care, you may notice other problems specific to your loved one. For instance, Alzheimer's disease and related disorders often alter the patient's sleep habits. You may even find that disturbing behavior increases at bedtime. To reduce the likelihood of insomnia, establish a regular schedule with a regular bedtime, help the patient get plenty of exercise, and make sure he uses the bathroom before going to bed.[8]

These are only a few of the examples of practical measures to consider. As you can see, caring for a dementia patient is more than a full-time job.

Sources of Help

Several care guides are available to help you through the practicalities. Some are listed in the endnotes for this chapter.

Beyond those, perhaps the most comprehensive guide, recommended in a publication produced by the American Association of Retired Persons (AARP) and the Alzheimer's Disease and Related Disorders Association (ADRDA), is titled *The 36-Hour Day*. Written by Nancy L. Mace and Peter V. Rabins, M.D., it covers every topic imaginable, defining dementia and outlining where to get help. It defines the characteristics and symptoms of dementia victims and describes the problems of independent living and daily care. In addition, it gives in-depth information regarding medical, behavioral, and emotional problems associated with dementia. It details outside resources and explains how dementia impacts the caregiver. Finally, it outlines financial and legal issues and explores nursing homes and other living arrangements.

For additional information, contact ADRDA at 919 N. Michigan Ave., Chicago, IL 60611. You can call at 312-335-8700, or if you want information about the ADRDA chapter nearest to you, you can call the toll-free phone number, 1-800-272-3900. In Illinois, the toll-free number is 1-800-572-6037.

Another possible source of help is the American Health Assistance Foundation (AHAF). This organization's primary purpose is to fund scientific research on age-related and degenerative diseases and to educate the public. It offers a variety of practical materials regarding glaucoma, heart disease, and stroke, in addition to Alzheimer's disease and related disorders.

Beyond that, through its Alzheimer's Family Relief Program, AHAF provides grants up to $500 directly to patients and their caregivers. The grants are designed to help cover emergency expenses related to the patient's care and treatment. Of course, applicants for this assistance must meet certain eligibility requirements.

For additional information regarding any of these services, contact AHAF by writing to 15825 Shady Grove Road, Suite 140, Rockville, MD 20850, or call 1-800-437-2423.

Special Notes to Caregivers

Emotional devastation often accompanies dementia, not just for the patient but also for his family. Those who are forced to watch a loved one slowly deteriorate often experience intense periods of mourning that may be more intense than that experienced at the patient's physical death.

Because of this emotional strain, it is crucial that you, as a caregiver, take care of yourself as well as your family member. Your sense of loss may deteriorate into a feeling of helplessness and even uselessness. It may finally degenerate to apathy, listlessness, perhaps irritability, and even a reduction of physical and mental stamina.

Safeguard your own health through proper nutrition and exercise and through regular medical checkups. *Don't be afraid to ask for help.* In fact, caregivers should develop an emergency plan outlining how the patient will receive care if the normal caregiver is sick or injured. Try to establish a support network.

And, if at all possible, join a support group. According to ADRDA (Alzheimer's Disease and Related Disorders Association), this step may be difficult at first. You may not be comfortable talking about your family's problems in dealing with a dementia patient. But the results are worth the risk. Your participation will prepare you for the present and for the future. It will provide encouragement and moral support. If you don't know of support groups in your area, call the toll-free ADRDA number listed in the previous section. Let someone help you.

And make use of other organizations that want to help you. In addition to ADRDA and the American Health Assistance Foundation (AHFA), the following organizations provide resources on dementia and help to caregivers:

National Institute on Aging,
National Institutes of Health
Public Information Office
Bethesda, MD 20892
  Information on Alzheimer's and related disorders is available by calling 1-800-438-4380.

American Association of Retired Persons
601 E St., NW
Washington, DC 20049
202-434-2277

National Council of Senior Citizens
1331 F St., NW.
Washington, DC 20004-1171
202-347-8800

National Council on the Aging, Inc.
409 Third St., SW., Suite 200
Washington, DC 20024
202-479-1200

Any state department of aging listed in Appendix B.

9

WHEN THE TIME COMES

Some of you seniors who have read every word up to now—especially about home care, life with the children, day care—may be convinced that none of these situations and possibilities for health provision is suitable for you.

The Choice Is Clear: A Nursing Home

You simply are too dependent for the suggested alternatives to work. And your caregiver and offspring agree. You together may have concluded, with heavy hearts, that the time has come to find a nursing home.

Try to get rid of the heavy heart, whether you're a senior or a caregiver. A future in a nursing home does not have to be devastating, even though it's uncharted ground for you and, as such, is loaded with fear of the unknown. It's scary, but it does not have to remain so. Lots of meaningful living can lie ahead.

If you're the child of an elder, remember: there is a

big difference between forcing a parent into a nursing home for selfish reasons and helping to place a parent there because it is indeed the best solution. So, if your motives are right, be at peace and walk your way through it.

Bob Butler said it well: "All of us have anxiety and fear about the possibility, when we grow old, of having to be put away in any institution, including a nursing home. It's understandable. What a just and effective society has to do is to create such outstanding policies and homes that that anxiety will evaporate in the face of high quality care."

He's holding up high standards, and rightly so. Approximately 1.5 million of the nation's elderly are currently living in nursing homes, and our television investigations in the eighties found that, shockingly, more than a third were substandard at that time. Recent evidence indicates progress against those conditions; however, a lot more is needed.

The *Washington Post,* for instance, reported in 1990 that of the 15,572 nursing homes treating Medicare or Medicaid patients, only 1.4 percent or 218 had been found guilty of mental or physical abuse. However, one quarter of all the homes surveyed reportedly "failed to keep residents clean, give drugs properly, or maintain isolation techniques to prevent infection. A third stored or served food improperly. One in seven didn't give prompt attention to residents who needed help eating or drinking. One in twenty failed to provide nursing services at all times." Improvement has been made, said

WHEN THE TIME COMES

Gail Wilensky of the Health Care Financing Administration, "but we have a lot of work to do."

Perhaps the greatest improvements in the quality of
nursing home care are the result of the Omnibus Budget Reconciliation Act (OBRA) of 1987—more specifically, the Nursing Home Reform Law. This law requires facilities to provide services such as nursing and
pharmacies as well as a level of care that would "promote maintenance or enhancement of the quality of life
of each resident." The law also clearly defines the training requirements for nurse's aides as well as the rights of
the residents of nursing homes.

Although we may have a considerable way to go as a
nation, the quality of care for our elderly *is* improving.
And I believe—as I said at the beginning—that you,
because you care, are going to find yourself better able
to carry out the task facing you than you thought. Care
and planning will make a great difference. You will be
able to find an appropriate home.

Begin the Discussion with Everyone

The best advice I can give to all concerned in this
process, once the signals indicate a nursing home is
necessary, is to make sure all the affected parties—the
family, the primary caregiver, and, most importantly,
the elder—are contributing to the discussion and the
planning.

The senior's view should be paramount, or nearly
so, and it should always be heard. Talk . . . and listen.

Ombudsmen Can Be Helpful

The best place to start is to make a connection quickly with a local ombudsman program or a citizen advocacy group. Ombudsmen are the state and local watchdogs of all nursing homes and will usually be an excellent source of information. Most often, they are associated with your Area Agency on Aging (see Appendix A). Their job is to investigate problems related to patient care and to be able to preserve and protect the rights of nursing home residents, the same rights everyone has. This should mean that they are informed and able to help those in the search for a home.

Map a Search Area

A smart, early step is to lay out a search area. Since drop-in visits are extremely important to nursing home residents, the children of an elderly parent should help choose a facility within an easy driving distance from their own home.

Spread out a road map of your area and draw a circle with, say, a twenty-five-mile radius, using your house as a center. Then try to confine your search to that area. Obviously, if you live in a large city, your circle could be much smaller, whereas if you're in a remote rural area, you may need to enlarge the radius. The point is to find a home that's within comfortable driving distance so your visits will be easy and regular.

If the parent has friends in the area, try to find a

home near a bus line. That way elderly friends who no longer drive can continue to visit.

Level of Care

At this point you should determine what kind of care your parent needs, and a personal physician or even a team of health care professionals should be invited into the assessment. The doctor or your local Office on Aging can put you in touch with a registered nurse trained to conduct what is called a home assessment. The nurse will visit with the elder and begin to answer a number of important questions:

• What is the patient's precise physical condition?

• To what extent can he or she manage the activities of daily living?

• Does he or she intend to apply for Medicaid?

Two Levels Available

The results of this gentle probing will clarify the specific kind of nursing home care needed. Generally, two levels of home care are available: intermediate care and skilled nursing care.

A nursing home offering intermediate care is for those seniors who can dress themselves and walk or be pushed in a wheelchair to a dining room. These facilities allow for independence while providing nursing supervision, protection, and assistance when needed.

Several concepts fall to some degree within the category of intermediate care short of the twenty-four-hour-a-day medical care and supervision facilities. According to the National Institute on Aging, they are found under such labels as

- *Residential care facilities,* providing room and board and possibly offering social, recreational, and spiritual programs.

- *Continuing care communities,* a relatively new concept, ensuring that all needs of the resident are met, including room and board, personal care and health care, and social activities.

- *Assisted living facilities,* which include retirement homes and board-and-care homes, with services differing from location to location but usually including meals, recreation, security, and assistance with walking, bathing, and dressing.

Skilled nursing, on the other hand, is for those who need a maximum level of around-the-clock nursing care. Usually a major health crisis sends people to a skilled nursing facility—perhaps a hip fracture, a stroke, a heart attack, or some other debilitating event. In those cases, the person cannot function without direct intervention on a twenty-four-hour basis.

Some facilities provide both intermediate and skilled-nursing levels of care, allowing residents to cross from one to the other. This service is called multilevel care and, once seniors are in the intermediate care section, they have guaranteed access to the skilled-nursing section.

As Dr. Butler explained, "Having the multilevel availability is so much better because we really don't like to keep moving people from one place to another. So, since life often leads to a change from one stage to another, if you can have all in the same physical plant, or closely related physical plant, these different stages of care are far preferable."

Big Homes, Small Homes

As you compile a list of homes in your mapped-out area that you want to consider, you definitely should include at least one multilevel facility on your first list.

You will find as you proceed that health care facilities come in everything from large-scale institutions to very small homes. Each extreme has advantages and disadvantages. While the large institutions, for example, can provide a more expensive staff and program, the small facilities may be homier and more suited to your taste.

One senior lady, interviewed in a small facility after a stay in a large nursing home, said, "You would hardly see the nurse twice, the same nurse, and it would take a long time before they would take care of you."

That, of course, is not the case in all homes. It might be that a medium-size home will strike a happy balance for you. But there was a time when small rural homes generated the least complaints of all types.

I recommend that in the initial stage of compiling potential homes for yourself or your parent that you consider facilities of various sizes to increase the chances of finding the one that's just right.

The Financial Factor

You must face one fact immediately: Nursing homes are expensive. The average cost is $83 a day for skilled nursing care, but in many parts of the country the cost rises as high as $125 a day.

Obviously, your finances will have a great influence upon your choice of a home, and this fact must be faced without sentiment and with a clear head.

"My husband died thinking that I would be well cared for," said one senior in a home, "but he didn't realize that nursing homes are very expensive. Now I am wiped out, and I'm on Medicaid."

Private Pay and Medicaid

The two common forms of payment are private pay —that's using your own money—or government assistance, usually in the form of Medicaid. It is important to remember that the entire health care sector, including such elements as Medicaid and Medicare, have been under study by the administration of President Clinton and by the Congress and will quite likely be changed considerably.

While most nursing homes today accept Medicaid as a form of payment, some do not. So if an elder will at some time require Medicaid acceptance, it is essential to choose a home that accepts this payment.

It is also important to realize as you plan that, even if you are wealthy and expect to make it on private pay, your needs may change or the home's rates may change, in which case you might need Medicaid quickly.

When you get down to talking to specific institutions, you should ask if they differentiate between a Medicaid bed and a private-pay bed. Nursing homes would much rather have the private-pay residents simply because without their payments nursing homes say they would not break even. Medicaid and Medicare payments usually fall below the actual cost of the care. Thus, if 65 percent of the facility's residents are Medicaid patients, the facility must rely on the remaining 35 percent, the private-pay residents, to make up the cost of operation.

As a result, some residents whose private-pay funds have run out were told they could not keep their bed and that no other bed was available. However, the Nursing Home Reform Law of 1987 restricts a facility's reasons for discharge of a resident, designating six specific causes for either discharge or transfer: welfare of the resident, improvement of the resident, health of others in the facility, safety of others, nonpayment, or closing of the facility. I will discuss this issue in greater detail in Chapter 11.

Take an Inventory of Resources

As early as possible in the process of choosing a nursing home, conduct an inventory of all financial resources, including pension or retirement income, real estate, savings accounts, stocks, bonds, and insurance benefits. Such an effort will help you immeasurably, both as you plan and also when and if you are required to report all pertinent financial information to the admissions director of the nursing home you choose.

The insurance most commonly associated with nursing home care has been Medicare. For long-term care, however, Medicare, in addition to its restrictions on the reasons for such care and on the type of facility, has offered only limited help because its benefits run out after one hundred days.

When the Medicare benefits run out, patients have turned most often to Medicaid, an often confusing program funded by both the federal and the state governments and administered by the states, with rules, eligibility requirements, and benefits varying state by state. Details of a state's Medicaid plan can be acquired from the state Health Care Association.

In 1992, The *Baltimore Sun* described America's condition in this sector of life quite clearly: "Medicaid has by default become the only substantial long-term care plan for a nation that critics say has failed to deal with the problem of long-term care for its elderly."

This $50-billion-plus problem will hopefully ease, and soon, as the country's best thinkers and activists come to grips with it at last.

Watch for Hidden Costs

When researching nursing homes, find out exactly what is covered in the monthly bill and what extra charges you can expect. For example, does the basic rate include medicines or physical therapy? Often there may be hidden charges.

One caregiver in the New York area found out about hidden costs the hard way. "When my grand-mother went in," she said, "we found that they charged for bedsore care, they charged for hand feeding, and it was really a rip-off."

A representative from a senior citizens law center said, "Nursing homes, I think, more and more fre-quently are limiting what is covered in their basic daily rate, and having what I call the *à la carte* method. Every service you get in the home is a separate charge. The basic rate is high enough—you really do need to know in advance, and you can ask them and they should provide you with a list of all the charges, all the extra services, and how much they charge for them. And they are required to give you notice when those charges are changing."

Long-term care insurance is one hope for the future

that is becoming increasingly available to cover both nursing home and home-care costs. Monthly premiums start at $2 for young people and rise to $600 or more for people in their seventies. Of course, it's a long-range matter. If you're looking for five or ten years in the future, it might be helpful, but you're not likely to be able to purchase a policy now that would protect you in a few years. This whole subject is under study and debate in Washington, and changes are expected.

Beware of Bribes

One other financial point to remember is that private donations given to assure places for seniors in nursing homes are nothing more than bribes, and they are illegal. Do not consider any facility suggesting this practice and report it immediately to the long-term care ombudsman for the state or to the state attorney general's office.

10

CHECK THEM OUT

N ow is the time for you, the primary caregiver, to undertake a bit of serious sleuthing on your own. It's better for the senior to let this early digging be done without him, simply to leave the wear and tear to someone he trusts. He can get in on the crucial matters later.

Make a Complete List

You, the child or caregiver, are now ready to make a list of nursing homes to investigate. Your state nursing home ombudsman and your Area Agency on Aging, as I indicated in the previous chapter, are the best places to obtain a complete list of local health-care facilities. Also your state health department keeps a current list of all homes county by county.

After assembling a full list, you should begin to talk to knowledgeable, trustworthy people to get opinions and advice. Clergy and doctors, especially your own, can be very helpful.

Val Halamandaris said, "The single best source, I believe, would be senior citizens and other family members that have been through a similar crisis."

Ready to Begin the Visits

With this kind of research, you can narrow your list to a handful of good homes within your desired geographical circle. The next job is to enlist reliable family members to visit every home in your area, still without the elder, since the task will be so exhausting. Make an appointment with the admissions director of each home and ask for an official tour.

When making the appointments, find out if there is a waiting list for each facility on your schedule. And do not be put off if there are such lists. Simply say, "I understand, but I would like to come by to see your facility, and I would like very much to receive your application."

This approach will allow you to see the home whether or not you're truly interested in it. The more information you have the better.

Furthermore, if you check a home with an excessively long waiting list and you like it, you may not want to disqualify it immediately. Waiting lists can change quickly, and a persistent person can sometimes speed the process. So if you really like a home, get on the waiting list and pursue it.

Be Emotionally Prepared

You, the child of an aging parent, would do well to pause a moment to reflect on what you're likely to see when you enter a nursing home, especially if you haven't visited one before. Most of us don't make such visits until we're down to the last excuse. Somehow we know that this is not the world we're used to.

So, remember, you won't feel comfortable. You'll feel embarrassed. You'll think you're standing out like a giant. Your voice will sound like a cannon in the quiet. Your movements will seem terribly fast.

Some of the people you see, or hear, will be very sick. Some will see very little with their eyes, staring vacantly ahead. Some will seem unaware of your presence, even when you pass within two or three feet. Some will mumble. Some may cry out.

But there will be people who are as bright and alert as you are. They will have lived a long time, but that alone will not stop them. An accident or serious illness may be slowing them drastically, but otherwise they're fine. They will speak and act like it too.

The point is to be prepared for the unexpected. You will feel alien, but you will overcome it. And it is important that you do so quickly. A lot is riding on you and your judgment.

Be Aware of Your Reception

Even though you will probably not be at your best at first, it is important that you take note of your reception. You will learn a lot about any home from the way you're treated, for that will give a clue as to the attitude and spirit of the place, and those elements say a lot about the way residents are treated.

Friendliness, openness, and warmth are obviously desirable. Pay attention to whether those qualities remain or are short-lived.

What to Look For

Common sense suggests that cleanliness is the first thing you'll notice when you're prospecting a home. Look at the structure of both buildings and furniture. Are they freshly painted, for example? Is the area free of dirt, debris, and vermin?

The staff is important too. Are there enough people to care for all the patients? Are there people moving around, doing their jobs? A lot of bustling activity in the hallways is generally a good sign, whether by staff or volunteers. And their spirit is important.

Do the patients seem happy? What do they look like? What expressions are on their faces? What might be in their thoughts?

Make a Checklist

You probably should have a checklist with you.

- Is the home clean and odor free?

- Is it well lighted and homelike?

- Are the residents' rooms attractive and filled with personal belongings? Are the residents allowed to bring their furniture and wall hangings with them?

- Are the rooms too hot or too cold? Do the rooms have individual thermostats?

- Are the bathrooms private, semi-private, or used by a number of residents? Walk into one or two to check for cleanliness.

- Is everything needed within reach in the rooms?

- Is an accessible nurse-call button in every room? Try one to see if it's working and how long it takes a nurse to answer.

- How do the residents look?

- Are most residents out of bed?

- Are they conversing with one another?

- Is their hair clean and combed?

- Are their hands and nails clean?

- Are their eyeglasses clean?

- Are the men shaved?

- Are the residents dressed well?

- Are they free of physical restraints?

- Are they alert rather than drowsy and perhaps overmedicated?

- Are the staff members courteous and pleasant, both to residents and to you?

- Do they seem to know the residents well?

- Is the ratio of residents to staff no more than 10 to 1?

- Do the nurse's aides—who usually deliver 90 percent of the care—show a good attitude?

- Is there an active physical therapy program, with a full-time therapist available to work with patients on a regular basis?

- How often and where is dental care provided?

- Are private TV sets allowed in the rooms, or are residents allowed to watch in a public sitting room?

- Do residents seem to have been placed in front of TV sets, even if they're not interested?

- Are residents allowed direct-line private telephones in their rooms?

- Are current newspapers and magazines on the tables?

- Is there a substantial schedule of innovative activities and outings?

- Is there a chaplaincy program and a pleasant place to worship for those to whom religion is important?

- What is the room-holding policy? Will rooms be held during periods of hospitalization or vacations?

- In cases of double rooms, what steps are taken to match up compatible roommates and to make changes if there are problems?

- If a resident does not like a room because of noise, distance from activities, or other reasons, how free is he to request and receive another room?

- Is there a residents' bill of rights and a residents' council that communicates grievances and special requests?

- How else does the home help residents exercise their rights?

The Importance of Mealtime

One of the most significant events in the life of a nursing home is mealtime, so the food program must be checked out thoroughly. Sit in on a meal.

First, of course, is the question of balanced nutrition. And you must observe the appearance, smell, and taste of the food that is served. And since mealtimes are truly the social event of the day, you should also investigate the dining room environment. Specifically check seating arrangements. Can residents change their seating, and is there a scheme for altering it for everyone on a regular basis?

Where Are the Residents?

If you don't see many residents, ask the tour guide to show you where they are. Ask to look at several floors. Often the quality of care can differ dramatically between floors, and some admissions directors will try to show you only a model floor.

Are Reports Posted?

Some states rate nursing homes, and if your state does, look to see if the home displays its official rating in a conspicuous place. Also notice whether the home posts inspection reports for all to see.

By this time, you should have a good idea what the home is like. You need to go through your entire list of homes in the same way. It's a time- and energy-consuming task, but all you can do is plod on until you are ready for the next step.

Second Visit: Talk to a Resident

On the basis of your initial impressions you should have been able to narrow down your list to just the homes that appear to be managed with care and excellence. The primary caregiver, probably a child of an elder, who's surveying the various facilities should now make a second visit. This time talk to a resident in each of the finalist homes and ask some of the same questions you posed to others earlier. You'll want to visit the resident alone and to ask questions in a setting to allow more thoughtful and considered answers.

A local rabbi or priest or minister—or perhaps a friend—can give you the name of a person in each home to visit.

Make your appointment directly with this resident and arrive at the nursing home unannounced. It is best if possible to make the visit in the evening on a weekend or a holiday to let you see the place when it's most likely to be short-handed. You should be able to observe quite a lot on your way to your host's room.

Keep It Confidential

Introduce yourself easily and naturally and explain that you want to ask some confidential questions about the facilities, hoping that the person will feel free to be candid. You should suggest, again naturally and easily, that you close the door while you chat.

Talk About Specifics

Keep in mind that this person lives there and is very dependent on the staff. She may be afraid to say anything critical, fearing retaliation. So avoid questions that are too general; be quite specific.

You might begin by finding out whether the staff is courteous. Ask about specific actions. Do they knock before entering? Do they respect the residents' privacy?

As on the earlier visits, it helps to have a list of questions for your interview:

• Is the mail sorted promptly and unopened?

• Is help offered to those who have difficulty reading or writing?

- Is the laundry well cared for? Are things ever lost or mixed up?

- Are medications handled in an orderly way?

- How difficult is it to get an appointment with the staff physician?

- Has she experienced or heard reports of theft from residents' rooms, especially by employees?

- Does she know of cases where employees use the residents' telephones behind their backs?

Fear and Guilt Can Arise

Once you have enough information on your own, you should involve your elder in the decision-making process. Make an appointment with the admissions officer for another tour.

And, don't forget, it's not uncommon for elders to be frightened and angry at this stage. They sense the time for a decision and a move drawing near.

One nursing home official described this tension with great compassion. "The people with whom I work," she said, "express feelings of loss, of anger at their situations, of grief at leaving a community and often of having to just part with things that they've gathered and loved all their lives. It's primarily a feeling of loss and often a feeling of fear, because they really don't know what the future holds for them."

And you, child or caregiver of the elderly, will probably begin to experience deeper guilt feelings than before. That's common, so don't let it throw you off track.

Dr. Butler made an interesting observation on this point: "I think the adult children of someone going into a nursing home are increasingly themselves in their sixties, because the average age of admission into a nursing home is about 81. So it rekindles many of the fears of age in the adult children, complicated by the possibility of some guilt and conflict: 'Why couldn't I have had the means—physical, emotional, or financial means—to have made it possible for Mom or Dad to stay at home?' That's tough."

This problem is serious enough that, in some homes, adult children belong to support groups that meet once a month to deal with the feelings of guilt.

The Admissions Interview

At the interview, the admissions staff will be looking to determine the exact nature of the senior's needs and his precise mental and physical condition. They will already have in hand the physician's assessment and the nurse's home assessment as to the level of care required. They will ask the senior such questions as: What do you do for yourself? Can you get out of bed yourself? Can you dress yourself?

I advise you and your elder to be as open and honest about any problems in previous living arrangements and any health-care problems that might seem minor to you. As much information as possible will make for a better admissions process.

Persistence Is Required

Once an application has been made, perhaps to more than one of the pool of homes selected, I also advise that the adult child not back off in his persistence to gain admission for his parent should there be a waiting list. Call each nursing home each week to check. Eventually a room will open, and a new chapter will begin.

Greater Emotion Likely

The emotion and trauma will probably intensify again, but don't lose sight of the point I made at the beginning: All of you are capable of passing through this.

Yes, it will be hard for most elders to say good-bye to their homes and make the transition to a new way of life. Many will simply not be able to understand, for a while, why they have to go to a nursing home. Intellectually they may know, but emotionally—it will take about two weeks for the trauma to pass and the settling-in and adjusting to occur.

Quality of Life

If you have done your homework well and have chosen a fine nursing home, settling in will happen more quickly and smoothly. And many seniors will soon be surprised by the quality of life they discover. Val Halamandaris talked about this surprise:

> I remember vividly meeting a man who was placed into a nursing home in Connecticut. The nursing home happened to be identified by our committee as one of the best in the country. And he said to me, "You know, until I was admitted into this nursing home, I never knew what it meant to live. It's strange to say it, but in the year and a half I've been in a nursing home I have learned what it really means to be a human being. There are other people who convinced me that I have some worth. I never felt that I was worth anything until I got here. I was given the kind of help and support and the love and the care and the affection I felt was important and necessary to me and, you know, I blossomed as an individual. It came rather late in my life, but I began to write, I began to paint, I began to do things. I only wish I could've had this care and this love and this support years ago."

Now's the Time for the Involvement of Many

Both caregiver and elder need to understand that in the right nursing home, which you can find if you are diligent, you both can begin to look forward to the years ahead. There is no reason why these years cannot be happy, fulfilling years, with many close moments left to share.

Remember, once the elder becomes a nursing home resident, it's time for the entire family to be real family. Family members should realize from the start that they will always have a place to turn to: the social services department of the facility. It's there for you. Use it.

A social services administrator of a home in Westchester County, New York, was quick to confirm this statement. "Our office is always open for family members to come in and have a laugh or a cry or whatever it happens to be, the necessity of today."

I want to impress upon all of you involved with an elder in a nursing home that this person is your advocate. Now is the time for the whole family to rally round. It is not the time to back away. The family and many friends must make a conscious effort to maintain contact because any elder, once inside an institution, has the very real fear of being forgotten.

On a broadcast segment about nursing homes some years ago, a resident gave me an answer to a question that haunts me even today. "Well, let's see," she said. "I

195

can't remember when I had the last visitor." Don't let that happen to your loved one!

Phone Calls and Visits

What a nursing home resident needs most of all are *regular telephone calls and visits that can be counted on*. I speak to all family members: Let your parent or relative know in advance when you plan to visit. And each time you go, take interesting things for this one you love— magazines, books, newspapers, special foods and treats, pictures of grandchildren and great-grandchildren.

If you can, set up a VCR and videotape family events. And take letters from family members far away, old family scrapbooks, and lots more.

You should also plan to take your elder on outings away from the facility and to bring him back to your home for occasional meals.

The Golden Years

These years can and should be golden years—content and secure with loved ones nearby. They should be filled with old memories and new experiences.

As in the case Val Halamandaris described, some seniors, after years of loneliness, will find that the transition to the community life of a health-related facility can be an invigorating and uplifting one. It can be the very opposite of what so many of them fear and dread.

For their families, it can open up an era of new security about the future.

It has been a series of hard choices, but your careful work throughout it all, and especially now, to ensure decent long-term health care has been worth the effort.

11

ELDERS HAVE
THEIR RIGHTS

Now that your elder is set nicely in a nursing home, neither the child/caregiver nor the elder should lose sight of some principles that increase in importance as change rolls in from every corner of the country.

Whether they're living at home, with children, or in a nursing home, senior citizens have the same rights all Americans have.

I'm certain many elders have not always been so sure about that statement, but the Older Americans Act, updated in 1987, serves as a legal reminder that elders are to be treated with the same dignity and are entitled to the same freedoms as all Americans.

Objectives for American Elders

This declaration of objectives states, "In keeping with the traditional American concept of the inherent dignity of the individual in our democratic society, the older people of our nation are entitled to:

1. An adequate income in retirement in accordance with the American standard of living.

2. The best possible physical and mental health that science can make available, regardless of the individual's economic status.

3. Suitable housing, selected by the individual, designed and located with reference to special needs and available at costs that older citizens can afford.

4. The same medical treatment offered to younger patients as well as adequate long-term care that sustains older people in their own communities and homes.

5. Opportunity for employment with no discriminatory personnel practices.

6. Retirement in health, honor, and dignity after years of contribution to the economy.

7. Participation in and contribution to meaningful activity within the widest range of civic, cultural, educational and training, and recreational opportunities.

8. Efficient and readily available community services, such as access to low-cost transportation.

9. Immediate benefit from proven research knowledge that can sustain and improve health and happiness.

10. Freedom, independence, and the free exercise of individual initiative in planning and managing their own lives, full participation in the planning and operation of community-based services and programs provided for their benefit, and protection against abuse, neglect, and exploitation.

The Older Americans Act serves as a guideline to the limitless opportunities our nation's elders have.

Rights of Nursing Home Residents

Furthermore, moving into a nursing home does not mean an elder is giving up his rights and freedoms as an American. He or she is still entitled to everything listed above. In fact, it is the responsibility of the nursing home to "promote and protect the rights of each resident," according to the act.

By federal law, the staff of the nursing home must go over the resident's rights with him. Some homes ask the resident to sign this "bill of rights." If the officials of the facility do not present these points automatically, you should ask them to. Always ask how they help residents exercise their rights.

Many nursing homes have a residents' council to serve as the voice of the nursing home residents. Make sure you ask whether such a group exists and, if so, how it operates.

A Summary of Rights

In summary, an elder's rights within a nursing home include:

- The right to choose a personal physician as well as the right to be fully informed in advance about care and treatment or any changes in care or treatment that may affect your well-being. This includes the right to participate in planning the care and treatment or changes in care and treatment. (There are exceptions to this right when a resident, such as an Alzheimer's patient, is judged incompetent.)

- The right to be free from physical or mental abuse, corporal punishment, involuntary seclusion, and any physical or chemical restraints imposed for purposes of discipline or convenience and not required to treat medical symptoms.

- The right to privacy with regard to accommodations, medical treatment, written and telephone communications, visits, and meetings of family and of resident groups. The right to privacy is all too frequently violated in institutional settings. You should watch to see if staff members maintain adequate privacy while administering treatment or bathing residents. Do they knock before entering a resident's room? Also note whether staff members discuss a resident's care or treatment in front of other residents.

- The right to confidentiality of personal and clinical records and the right of access to current clinical records of the resident upon request by the resident or the resident's legal representative. State laws usually limit the automatic release of medical information to a few specific situations, such as releases to other professionals for diagnostic purposes.

- The right to accommodation of needs, including the right: (a) to reside and receive services with reasonable accommodations of individual needs and preferences, except where the health or safety of the individual or other residents would be endangered, and (b) to receive notice before the room or roommate of the resident in the facility is changed. Although not mentioned specifically in the residents' rights, the facility is obligated by the Nursing Home Reform Amendments to provide individualized care and treatment.

- The right to voice grievances—without discrimination or reprisal—with respect to treatment or care that is (or fails to be) furnished, plus the right to prompt efforts by the facility to resolve grievances. These include any grievances regarding the behavior of other residents.

- The right to organize and participate in resident groups in the facility and with the families of other residents in the facility.

- The right to participate in social, religious, and community activities that do not interfere with the rights of other residents.

- The right to examine, upon reasonable request, the results of the most recent survey of the facility conducted by the Secretary [of Health and Human Services] or the State, plus any plan of correction.

- The right to quality care. A nursing facility must establish and maintain identical policies and practices regarding transfer, discharge, and the provision of services required under the state's Medicaid plan for all individuals *regardless of source of payment.*

- The right to equal treatment in regard to admissions practices, whether the resident intends to apply for Medicare or Medicaid or to pay expenses with private funds. Under the Medicare/Medicaid Anti-Fraud Abuse Amendments, a person or organization that violates any part of this provision is subject to criminal prosecution.

- The right to remain in the facility and refuse transfer or discharge. The following situations are exceptions:

  a. When transfer or discharge is necessary to meet the resident's welfare and the resident's welfare cannot be met in the facility.

  b. When transfer or discharge is appropriate because the resident's health has improved sufficiently so that the resident no longer needs the services provided by the facility.

  c. When the safety of individuals in the facility is endangered.

  d. When the health of individuals in the facility would otherwise be endangered.

  e. When the resident has failed, after reasonable notice, to pay an allowable charge imposed by the facility for an item or service requested by the resident and for which the resident may be charged above the basic rate.

  f. When the facility ceases to operate.

  (Regardless of reason, the facility must notify the resident and, if known, a family member or legal representative of the transfer or discharge at least 30 days in advance.)

- The right to sufficient preparation and orientation to ensure safe and orderly transfer or discharge from the facility.

- The right to notice of bed-hold period in the event that a resident is transferred for hospitalization or therapeutic leave.

- The right to priority readmission when the resident's leave for medical reason exceeds the bed-hold period paid for under the state Medicaid plan and if, at the time of readmission, the resident requires the services provided by the facility.

- The right to be informed, at the time the resident becomes eligible for medical assistance, of the items and services that are included in nursing facility services under the state plan, and of items and services offered by the facility for which the resident may be charged and the amount of charges. The resident also has the right to be informed of any changes in the items and services or in charges imposed.

- The right to manage personal income. Residents do not have to sign their income over to the home automatically. However, having a power of attorney prepared as a backup is a good idea. If the resident chooses to turn income over to the facility, the facility must assure a full and complete separate accounting of each such resident's personal funds, maintain a written record of all financial transactions involving the personal funds of a resident deposited with the facility, and afford the resident reasonable access to such record.

• The right to be informed about rights. The nursing facility must inform each resident, orally and in writing at the time of admission, of the resident's legal rights during the stay at the facility.

If you have questions about any of these rights, be sure to ask the administration of the home to go over them with you, since some homes still neglect certain portions of the Nursing Home Reform Law of 1987. The resident and his family have the right to stay informed of everything regarding the stay in the nursing home.

Quality of Life Guaranteed

According to federal law, skilled nursing facilities, particularly those certified by Medicaid and Medicare, must insure that the conditions of residents do not diminish. The law clearly states that "a nursing facility must care for its residents in such a manner and in such an environment as will promote maintenance or enhancement of the quality of life of each resident."

As a result of the Nursing Home Reform Law of 1987, many nursing homes have improved the quality of their care. However, others still refuse to make the necessary changes. When seeking a nursing home, be sensitive to the warning signs of such a facility. The most significant warning, as I've indicated, is the condition of the patients themselves. Are they out of bed? Is their appearance neat? Are they well dressed? Are they alert? Are they active? Or are the majority of residents still in their rooms? And, most importantly, how are the staff treating the residents?

If you have concerns about a facility, contact your local ombudsman. His responsibility is to see that the rights of nursing home residents are being acknowledged and respected.

Flagrant Examples of Abuse

Despite the promises, an investigation by ABC News' "20/20" uncovered in 1991 sickening, dismaying examples of flagrant elder abuse in Texas nursing homes that challenged one's belief in the basic goodness of human beings.

And this abuse is what must be guarded against in the selection process at all costs. Let me say quickly, however, that the percentage of good homes is high, and many are outstanding. Furthermore, regulation and oversight continue to improve, and I am optimistic about the future. But caution by families and caregivers is critical, and you must be quick to report any violations of federal and state laws for elders.

In the Texas cases, we found patient dignity to be an unknown concept. Residents were treated with callousness bordering on barbarism. We found patients tied to chairs and bound to beds, unwashed, uncared-for, and unwanted.

Katherine Bates, chief executive of United People for Better Nursing Home Care, told us on camera about the condition of her mother in a nursing home. She "had on a full, flowing gown, and it was just covered and stained with everything you can imagine, every secretion from a human's body."

She continued, "I found a bedsore that I could stick my hand in. Boy, she really had maggots in there. And that is a horrible thing, to think that someone that has taken care of you and been so concerned for you all her life ends up in an institution like that, where, if it were an animal, people wouldn't allow it."

One resident said the food she was fed was slop. "I wouldn't feed it to a dog," she said.

Others spoke of not getting enough to eat, and one nurse told us that a resident's entire meal might consist of only a bowl of thin soup.

The obvious explanation for the abuses—greed—lay in the fact that a nursing home receives federal dollars for every Medicaid patient. The home uses the money to take care of the patient and what is left over is profit. The less care, the more profit.

To summarize the heartbreaking report, findings included thievery, agonizing pain, filth, roaches and ants crawling on patients, sewage leaking into a food preparation area, and even death by neglect.

Among the saddest discoveries was widespread misdiagnosis of Alzheimer's disease, with patients being placed on strong drugs that robbed them of any chance to participate in life. "They are treated as if nothing further can be done and, as a result, it becomes a self-fulfilling prophecy," said one worker.

The Texas Health Care Association, questioned about the report, said the homes in the state were not as bad as portrayed. Nonetheless, although the correspondent in the story was careful to note that there were exceptions to those homes covered, that did not diminish the reality of the widespread abuse in numerous homes. Texas governor Ann Richards promised a complete overhaul of the nursing home system and recent reports are encouraging.

Other Kinds of Abuse

For most of you reading this book, if you encounter problems they're likely to be much less severe than those just described. But you need to be aware that abuse can occur in many forms and in different places.

Outside of the nursing home, the elderly are often victims of financial exploitation, including door-to-door con men and phone scams.

More than 140,000 cases of widely varying elder abuse are reported each year. However, many advocates of the elderly believe more than 2 million reportable cases occur each year, an estimate that has more than doubled in the last ten years.

What prevents senior citizens from reporting abuse? Many of them feel the justice system is not sensitive to their needs. They may be intimidated by the courts. And some simply feel a sense of shame at being conned.

In some areas, attorneys and authorities are working to make the courts more accessible to elders. The purpose of such activities is to recognize senior citizens as *citizens,* with the right to justice. And certainly that includes the right to *preventive* justice.

Should You Hire an Attorney?

Problems of abuse are not the only reasons for considering legal assistance. Life for everyone, including the elderly, becomes more complicated each year. As a caregiver, you probably should have a lawyer available, especially as you and your elder begin making the decision about a nursing home and then deal with the many extraordinary legal issues encountered by the elderly. For example, a lawyer can assist with the frequently changing laws of governmental programs. If finances make it difficult for you to afford a lawyer, several options are available, including legal service offices and reduced-fee lawyer referral services.

A Will Is Crucial

While it may be difficult to discuss, be sure your elder has drawn up a will. This ensures that she has control over her assets. Without a will, an entire estate, no matter how big or small, might end up in the hands of the state rather than the family.

Different types of wills, such as handwritten or fill-in-the-blank wills, are legal in some states. However, lawyers are up to date on state laws and can help put together a more personalized estate plan.

Although it is not an alternative to a will, the living will is also important. It is a signed, dated, witnessed document in which the elder states his wishes about the use of life-sustaining procedures during a terminal illness. Signing a living will while competent gives a person the power to let his wishes be known. You can also leave this decision to a trusted friend or family member.

Trusts Are Popular

The trust has become more popular over the last fifty years. It involves the transfer of property to a trustee, who then invests it and manages it for the trust's beneficiaries. The beneficiary can be anyone the creator of the trust chooses, including himself. Trusts are not designed only for the extremely wealthy; people of modest means find them helpful.

An elder may want to consider a trust for several reasons: (1) avoiding the probate process at the time of death, (2) lessening the tax burden on the family and the estate, and (3) managing property.

A trust may serve to protect an elder, the property

owner, from his own indiscretions or incompetence as he grows older.

The Sharing of Power

A senior may also want to consider joint ownership of his accounts with one of his children. That way he will have someone to pay bills and deposit checks. A lawyer can advise you about potential problems with such an arrangement.

Guardianship is a painful process in which the court declares an adult incompetent and appoints a guardian to manage his affairs. Since guardianship is a complicated process, always consult a lawyer.

When an elder gives the power of attorney, the power to do business on his behalf, to a child or spouse, it sounds almost as if he is signing his life away. But remember, a power of attorney can be limited to a specific situation. For example, if he needs a one-time project completed, such as selling a house or handling a bank account, the power of attorney can be restricted to that one task.

Keep in mind that while standard power of attorney forms can be purchased at a stationery or office supply store, an elder might be wiser to have his lawyer draw up the document. Lawyers can customize it to specific needs. For example, an elder may not want the power of attorney to go into effect unless she becomes mentally incompetent.

Helen Hayes
Defied Prejudices

*W*ithout trying, *Helen Hayes defied the
great prejudices that often hit older women
with a double measure of unfairness. Of
course, she was enormously talented and
worked hard and long well into her late
years. She certainly was one of the
outstanding actresses of our time. She simply
refused to consider herself old and worn out.
For that, all of us admire her.*

*But the quality I find most striking in
this lady was her great beauty—particularly
in her late years. I would see her and I
would think, "She is beautiful." Yes, toward
the end of her life she was "old," but she
was beautiful.*

Everyone I know thought that. And that, unhappily, is quite rare with women in this day when youth (and youth only) is thought beautiful. On the other hand, people sometimes see older men and think, "His gray hair is so attractive and mature." Occasionally, advancing age in men is said to be sexy.

So it's a double prejudice with older women. They're old. *That draws prejudice. And they're old* women. *That draws even more prejudice.*

But not so with Helen Hayes. People looked at her and they saw a beautiful person, no matter what age. I didn't know her well, but I'm convinced her beauty radiated from within, fed by activity and, yes, attitude. In her words, she was not a senior citizen but a maturian.

Burial Plans

As the child of an older adult, you will find that one of the most difficult things to do for your parent is to make prearranged funeral plans. You will suddenly find yourself face to face with your parent's mortality—and your own.

My suggestion is that you listen carefully for any hint of a parent's wishes in the matter and then cooperate with that. If the parent has never mentioned it, bringing up the subject out of the blue will almost certainly give an impression of hustling an ancestor off to the mortuary. It really is doubtful that it would be well received.

If the older adult has never made mention of a desire to prearrange his funeral, then any planning you do had best remain secret. However, prearranging funeral plans will make things much easier down the road. Once the prearrangements are paid for, the funeral is guaranteed.

When you make the arrangements with the funeral home, be sure you know what you're paying for. What is included in the price and what isn't? For example, the price of cemetery plots often can't be guaranteed because prices change so rapidly.

The Federal Trade Commission's Funeral Industry Practices Trade Regulation Rule, or the FTC Funeral Rule, requires the funeral provider to inform you in advance of (1) the costs of all funeral goods and services you will be paying for and (2) which of these goods and services are not required by state and local law. Make sure you have all of this information in writing. For more specific information, contact the Federal Trade Commission.

When you make prearranged plans, the funeral home, under approval of the state, puts the money into a trust. Again, your parent can make these plans or you can do it for her. If the trust is revocable, she will still have control over the funds. However, this also means that the trust is counted as an asset.

People who want to qualify for Medicaid often transfer this money into an irrevocable trust. In some states, Medicaid will allow a participant to put up to $10,000 aside for prearranged funeral plans. When this fund is irrevocable, it is not considered an asset. And the interest that accrues compensates for the inflation of funeral costs.

Irrevocable trusts are often a protection from nursing home costs. Without an irrevocable trust, or irrevocable burial plans, many elderly are forced to use the money set aside for burial plans to pay for nursing home care before they can qualify for Medicaid. Their families are then stressed to find the resources to cover the funeral.

Therefore, at the time you make prearranged funeral plans, it is wise to decide whether you and your parent want to put the money into an irrevocable trust. For, in many states, Social Services, when determining if your parent can qualify for Medicaid, can check back a few years to see how your parent's money has been spent. If your parent wrote you a check for $5,000 within the period that Social Services can check, and the money was not put into an irrevocable trust, you will be required to use that $5,000 to fund nursing home expenses before Medicaid begins coverage.

In some states, Social Services will tell people to be sure their funeral plans are irrevocable before they fill out the paper work.

Funeral planning is a difficult subject to deal with. But when all the paper work is done, you (and your parent) will feel much more secure.

Work to Stay Informed

As in every situation, your best protection is knowledge. Older Americans should be aware of the Older Americans Act, which as I mentioned earlier, simply recognizes that you are still to be treated as a citizen of the United States. When entering a nursing home, you should be certain that you and your family understand the residents' rights. And you should see to it that they are exercised throughout the facility.

When visiting a parent in the nursing home, children should ask the parent questions: "Are you happy?" "How are you being treated?" Be aware of any unusual changes.

Some call it a gut feeling, others call it intuition, but a concerned family member is usually sensitive to the "spirit" of a nursing facility. You are probably also sensitive to your parent's needs and wants.

Remember that the majority of nursing facilities have very good standards. And be confident that you can know whether a situation is good for your parent.

12

THE FUTURE
IS SERIOUS

As I wind down my efforts in this book to help you (elders and children of elders) make some important decisions about long-term health care, I would be remiss not to turn your thinking toward the serious issues facing us as a nation and, indeed, as a world.

In the United States we have 31 million people 65 years of age and older—12 percent of the population. The National Institute on Aging says the figure will be 20 percent by the year 2025. We have only to look at the rise in average life expectancy in this country from 35 in 1776 to 75 today to understand why this percentage is increasing.

Senior citizens are increasing faster by far than any other segment of the population, and they are using more and more of America's health-care dollars.

Pepper Used
Savvy and Insight

I admired Claude Pepper for many years as he combined political savvy and knowledge of the Washington community with insights into gerontology and geriatric medicine to work with rare effectiveness for senior citizens.

The Florida Congressman continued his aggressive service of older people well into his nineties, using every instrument available to keep driving ahead—trifocals, twin hearing aids, a pacemaker. He refused to be put on the shelf himself, and he battled for the same rights for others.

One of my most memorable times with the congressman came when he and I saw a television commercial that was especially deplorable in its prejudice against seniors. It depicted a family that included an older man who was hard of hearing, and the ad made fun of him in a way that would have offended everyone and generated an avalanche of protest mail had the man been younger. It played on the myth that all older people are hard of hearing and it's okay to make fun of them.

Pepper got on the phone right there, talked to some people, and got the commercial taken off the air and changed.

Seniors need more champions like Claude Pepper. He knew what he was doing, and he had courage.

Generational Collision

These facts have put us on a generational collision course. Younger people are raising profound questions about the justice of our division of the health-care pie. They make arguments about paying a high percentage of their incomes to Social Security when fewer than 30 percent of them expect to use Social Security. Furthermore, some say, the elderly have been prospering more than any other group and should be prepared to sacrifice a bit.

The last contention is not altogether accurate, however, since income and assets are not evenly distributed among the elderly, but rather are highly concentrated among the "rich old." In this affluent nation, only slightly more than 5.5 percent of older people have incomes above $50,000 a year. On the whole, the old are the poorest of adults.

Regardless, the disagreements will get worse and solutions will not come easily. But fairness must prevail, and that can be a mushy concept in heated battle. What *is* a fair share for elders of scarce health-care dollars? The answer is there somewhere, and it must be found.

Autonomy and Justice

Ethicists are properly concerned about the clash that flows from the issue of health care apportionment. Professor Harry R. Moody, deputy director of the Brookdale Center on Aging, helped stir my thinking on the matter when he spoke of the inevitable collision of two compelling liberal ideas, autonomy and justice. Think of autonomy (the rights, the entitlements, the quality of life) in terms, for example, of the long-term care of the 1.5 million Americans in nursing homes. Then think of the justice between generations in a nation where 33 percent of all health-care expenditures goes to just 12 percent of the population.[1]

Americans of every age must involve themselves in the dilemma posed by this conflict between rights and justice for all. Will the rights of elders in nursing homes be upheld? Think about it: the right to respect and self-determination, the right to refuse treatment, the right to privacy, the right to be taken care of in the least restrictive environment, and ultimately even the right to die. Or will the rights of children and future generations rise up, to the detriment of the elderly?

The issue is not abstract, for the numbers will certainly grow; a political collision and perhaps explosion are approaching. We will need the wisdom of Solomon.

Compassion Must Be Part of the Solution

It strikes me that some rights of all *can* be curtailed and must be if we are to protect all. A crucial word—even if it sounds corny—is *compassion*. Obviously, the elderly must not be cut off, but neither must the younger generations be ignored. Justice, it seems, must have an element of compassion or it isn't just. We have seen times in history when that element was ignored, and brutality resulted. But it doesn't have to be that way. Surely, reasoning that protects all to the fullest extent possible can be found by sincere, compassionate thinking.

We will need the best minds in the nation to grapple with this and other eldercare problems. None must shirk the responsibility.

Elders Are Often Ignored

The controversy spills over into other areas, particularly noticeable to me as I have deepened my interest in gerontology and geriatric medicine in the last dozen or more years. For example, Dr. Robert N. Butler, whom I've mentioned several times because of his importance to my education on these matters, has spoken and written considerably on "ageism," a term he coined in 1968 and which he defined this way:

> Ageism can be seen as a systematic stereotyping of and discrimination against people because they are old, just as racism and sexism accomplish this with skin color and gender. Old people are categorized as senile, rigid in thought and manner, old-fashioned in morality and skills. . . . Ageism allows the younger generation to see older people as different from themselves; thus they subtly cease to identify with elders as human beings.[2]

THE FUTURE IS SERIOUS

It should be remembered that Butler has been just as concerned with older people's negativism toward young people. And, happily, he believes ageism as a disease infecting both groups can be treated.

Furthermore, he points out, the intergenerational conflict does not actually embrace the views of people at large, who are found in national polls to want elders to maintain (or expand) their entitlements.

Nonetheless, if the surge in ageism—the outright discrimination leveled against seniors—is not overcome, it could prevent progress toward the development of policies and practices that enhance life, medically and otherwise, for elders in America.

Medical Profession Criticized

One of the concerns, for example, voiced in the generational controversy has criticized the medical profession for its attitude toward elders. A major report by *U.S. News & World Report* in January 1993 found that:

- Many old people don't get the screening tests they should.

- Doctors tend to overload elderly people with unnecessary pills or, conversely, fail to prescribe needed medications.

- Surgeons either rush old patients into futile or harmful surgery or throw in the towel prematurely on the assumption that they won't pull through anyway.

- For a host of lab tests commonly ordered on elderly people, "normal" results remain undefined, making it difficult to separate symptoms of disease from signs of increasing age.

- Only now are the elderly being included in research trials, which doctors rely on to formulate treatment plans.

Agreeing with Butler's earlier writings about the fact that few medical school graduates enter the geriatrics field, the report said that only eight of the nation's 126 medical schools require separate courses in geriatric medicine.

"In fact," Butler said, "on the whole, physicians do not invest the same amount of time in dealing with elderly patients as they do in their younger counterparts. Doctors question why they should even bother treating certain problems of the aged; after all, the patients are old. Is it worth treating them? Their problems are irreversible, unexciting, and unprofitable."[3]

Reason for Hope

With warnings like those sounded over the years by several in the national press, by numerous experts typified by Butler, Moody, Halamandaris, and by political and moral leaders like the late Claude Pepper, progress has been made on numerous fronts, but much is left to do, especially among the younger generations, who make strong cases. It is too soon to tell whether changes in federal leadership will make significant differences quickly. The wheels of Congress and bureaucracy move slower and slower, it seems.

I have been concerned for some time that no readily apparent figure has risen up to provide the aggressive and powerful leadership of Congressman Pepper. Many strong men and women work tirelessly on behalf of elders, but the faithful, clear voice of the unwavering Floridian is missed.

We Need Harmony

As I said in the introduction, government money is not the only answer to the health-care needs of elders nor to the health-care needs of the populace in general. Rather, intelligent reasoning, unselfishness, planning, and policymaking are the vital first ingredients. The nation needs harmony and togetherness on this and all issues as it never has before.

We have wandered into a smothering atmosphere of special interest, materialism, and short-sightedness— sometimes appropriately called "gridlock"—that simply won't do in a nation with the underlying principles and integrity of this one.

One is inevitably driven back to the words of "Union . . . justice . . . tranquility . . . common

defense . . . general welfare . . . blessings of lib-
erty" as we confront stalemate and stagnation in matters
deeply affecting the people.

We have before us the fruit of excruciatingly hard
work by scientific, medical, nutrition, and research
people in untold fields to improve the lives of humans at
every stage and level, with a concomitant result of extending health and life into ever-lengthening years. We
have been *very* successful—so much that we've run into
problems of what to do with our success.

It would be the ultimate silliness to let the problems
triumph.

Flashes of Great Expectation

We have moments even now, flashes, when you can
almost see the time when we'll have no "elderly problem," a time when everyone knows *age* is not a dirty
word, a time when mistreatment and misunderstanding
of older people is an anachronism.

We will know that there is no fixed timetable for
decline of powers or impairment of faculties. Sure,
there is a difference between a 40-year-old and someone who has reached 85. But the difference does not
always say, "I'm more valuable, or more capable, or
more reliable than you are." Sometimes it says, "I've
lived longer than you have and been more exposed to
accident and disease," or maybe even, "The forces of
years have left some of my systems a little less efficient."

Similarly, the difference never looks the opposite

direction and says, "You're just a kid and haven't earned the right to be heard."

Even in those flashes of great expectation, we know that some who live many years will encounter poor health, injury, poverty, and loneliness. This needn't, however, be automatically attributed to longevity and thus ignored or belittled. It needn't be the norm to say, "I'm sorry; that's the way it is when you get old."

Yes, there's an improving picture ahead if we as a society want it. The only obstacles are myth, injustice, and prejudice. And I believe we can remove them.

APPENDIX A

Finding the Help
You Need

Throughout this book, I have stressed that in your attempt to maintain independence or to care for an aging loved one you don't have to "go it alone." Now we come to the nuts and bolts. How can you find the help you need?

An organization called Children of Aging Parents (CAPS), located in Levittown, Pennsylvania, offers several suggestions to lead you through the process of researching the resources available to you.

CAPS suggests that you begin with your local phone book—particularly the blue pages. Look through the *Human Services* section to get an overall picture of the agencies and organizations serving your area. The local library is another good place to find information—especially if you look under headings such as *Senior Services, Aging, Human Services,* etc. And don't forget about public officials. You pay them. Their job is to serve you.

Beyond that, you may want to contact your state department on aging, located in your state capital. I have provided a list of these agencies in Appendix B. They can lead you to a host of statewide services and can connect you with services in your area.

Within your community, CAPS says you should consider these options for gaining additional information:

Area Agency on Aging (AAA) I have mentioned this resource throughout this book. "Triple A's" offer a host of programs for the elderly and their families. The programs vary from community to community, but they include services that help with transportation, shopping, telephone reassurance, and care management. Often these services are provided at no charge to elderly people with low incomes.

Every county or geographic area in the country has a "Triple A," probably several. New York has dozens, ranging from the American Automobile Association to Triple A Yacht Charters. What you want is the Area Agency on Aging listing. If you are unable to find this in your local phone book, contact your local operator, your State Association of Area Agencies on Aging, or the National Association of Area Agencies on Aging (1112 16th St., NW, Suite 100, Washington, DC 20036, or call 202-296-8130). Or call the Eldercare Locator at 1-800-677-1116.

Visiting or Community Nurses Association Local nurses know your community, and they are used to talking with elderly people. In addition to their ability to provide in-home medical services, they may be able to advise you concerning issues like reimbursement eligibility.

Social Security Office The Social Security Administration has over 1,300 offices nationwide. Employees at your local Social Security office can explain government benefits for health care. Often they also have information regarding local care options such as hospice. If you need additional help, you can call the Social Security Administration's toll free number at 1-800-772-1213.

Hospital Social Service or Education Departments Hospital social workers specialize in developing discharge care plans. Because of the nature of their work, they tend to have current information on services available within the community.

Information and Referral or Crisis Hotlines Trained telephone consultants may be available in your community to guide you through your particular situation. They can help you determine your needs, even those you haven't considered yet, and they can suggest resources to meet them.

American Red Cross Your local chapter of the Red Cross has a vast number of resources. You may even find that it offers a special course in home health care skills.

Family Service Agency This type of organization employs professionals who view the family as a unit. They offer a broad concern for each family member's welfare, and they are available to help you sort through the problems of your unique situation.

Neighborhood Senior Center Services available at senior centers all across the United States are designed for the elderly and their families. In some localities, the senior center actually is the "point of access" to the entire care system for elderly people. When you call, ask to talk with the Client Services Supervisor.

Church and Synagogue Outreach Ministries Religious organizations tend to be very helpful to the elderly and their families, especially if the family has been a familiar part of the fellowship. Among other services, they often sponsor caregiver support groups of various kinds.

Mental Health Association This organization offers counselors, someone to talk to. CAPS notes, "You are not going crazy if you break into tears; you need help dealing with stress."

Private Geriatric Care Consultant If your community is fortunate enough to have this type of specialist, he or she can save you a lot of worry, as well as research time, and sometimes money. Usually their services are well worth the fee. But remember, to date there are no general standards of practice, so try to get recommendations from others in your community.

Gerontology Departments of Universities People who need help tend to overlook these resources, but they can offer a tremendous array of information.

In addition to these resources, we offer the following directories of agencies that can provide specific information. Research and preparation is the key to success. Don't be afraid to ask questions.

APPENDIX B

National Association of State Units of Aging

The following is a directory of units on aging at the state level. The listing was provided by the National Association of State Units on Aging (NASUA). If you are unable to contact your state agency, or if you have further questions regarding the national organization, you can contact NASUA at 1225 I Street, NW, Suite 725, Washington, DC 20005, or call 202-785-0707.

ALABAMA
Commission on Aging
RSA Plaza, Suite 470
770 Washington Ave.
Montgomery, AL 36130
205-242-5743

ALASKA
Older Alaskans Commission
Department of Administration
Pouch C, Mail Station 0209
Juneau, AK 99811-0209
907-465-3250

ARIZONA
Aging and Adult Administration
Department of Economic Security
1789 W. Jefferson, #950A
Phoenix, AZ 85007
602-542-4446

ARKANSAS
Division of Aging & Adult Services
Arkansas Department of Human Services
P.O. Box 1437, Slot 1412
7th and Main Sts.
Little Rock, AR 72201
501-682-2441

CALIFORNIA
Department of Aging
1600 K St.
Sacramento, CA 95814
916-322-5290

COLORADO
Aging and Adult Service
Department of Social Services
1575 Sherman St., 4th Fl.
Denver, CO 80203-1714
303-866-3851

CONNECTICUT
Department on Aging
175 Main St.
Hartford, CT 06106
203-566-3238

DELAWARE
Division on Aging
Department of Health & Social Services
1901 N. DuPont Hwy.
New Castle, DE 19720
302-577-4791

DISTRICT OF COLUMBIA
Office on Aging
1424 K St., NW, 2nd Fl.
Washington, DC 20005
202-724-5626

FLORIDA
Department of Elder Affairs
Building 1, Rm. 317
1317 Winewood Blvd.
Tallahassee, FL 32301
904-922-5297

GEORGIA
Office of Aging
878 Peachtree St. NE, Rm. 632
Atlanta, GA 30309
404-894-5333

GUAM
Division of Senior Citizens
Department of Public Health & Social Services
Government of Guam
P.O. Box 2816
Agana, Guam 96910
011-671-734-4361

HAWAII
Executive Office on Aging
Office of the Governor
335 Merchant St., Rm. 241
Honolulu, HI 96813
808-586-0100

IDAHO
Office on Aging
Rm. 108, Statehouse
Boise, ID 83720
208-334-3833

ILLINOIS
Department on Aging
421 E. Capitol Ave.
Springfield, IL 62701
217-785-2870

INDIANA
Bureau of Aging/In Home Services
402 W. Washington St., #E-431
Indianapolis, IN 46207-7083
317-232-7020

IOWA
Department of Elder Affairs
Jewett Bldg., Suite 236
914 Grand Ave.
Des Moines, IA 50319
515-281-5187

KANSAS
Department on Aging
Docking State Office Bldg., 122-S
915 SW Harrison
Topeka, KS 66612-1500
913-296-4986

KENTUCKY
Division of Aging Services
Cabinet for Human Resources
275 E. Main St., 6 West
Frankfort, KY 40621
502-564-6930

LOUISIANA
Office of Elderly Affairs
P.O. Box 80374
4550 N. Blvd., 2nd Fl.
Baton Rouge, LA 70806
504-925-1700

MAINE
Bureau of Elder & Adult Services
Department of Human Services
State House, Station #11
Augusta, ME 04333
207-624-5335

MARYLAND
Office on Aging
State Office Building, Rm. 1004
301 W. Preston St.
Baltimore, MD 21201
410-225-1100

MASSACHUSETTS
Executive Office of Elder Affairs
1 Ashburton Pl., 5th Fl.
Boston, MA 02108
617-727-7750

MICHIGAN
Office of Services to the Aging
P.O. Box 30026
Lansing, MI 48909
517-373-8230

MINNESOTA
Board on Aging
444 Lafayette Rd.
St. Paul, MN 55155-3843
612-296-2770

MISSISSIPPI
Council on Aging
Division of Aging and Adult Services
421 W. Pascagoula St.
Jackson, MS 39203-3524
601-949-2070

MISSOURI
Division on Aging
Department of Social Services
P.O. Box 1337
615 Howerton Ct.
Jefferson City, MO 65102-1337
314-751-3082

MONTANA
Governors' Office on Aging
State Capitol Bldg.
Capitol Station, Rm. 219
Helena, MT 59620
406-444-3111

NEBRASKA
Department on Aging
P.O. Box 95044
301 Centennial Mall, South
Lincoln, NE 68509
402-471-2306

NEVADA
Division for Aging Services
Department of Human Resources
340 N. 11th St., Suite 114
Las Vegas, NV 89101
702-486-3545

NEW HAMPSHIRE
Division of Elderly & Adult Services
State Office Park South
115 Pleasant St., Annex Bldg. #1
Concord, NH 03301-3843
603-271-4680

NEW JERSEY
Division on Aging
Department of Community Affairs
CN 807
S. Broad and Front Sts.
Trenton, NJ 08625-0807
609-292-4833

NEW MEXICO
State Agency on Aging
La Villa Rivera Bldg.
224 E. Palace Ave., 4th Fl.
Santa Fe, NM 87501
505-827-7640

NEW YORK
Office for the Aging
New York State Plaza
Agency Bldg. #2
Albany, NY 12223
518-474-4425

NORTH CAROLINA
Division of Aging
CB 29531
693 Palmer Dr.
Raleigh, NC 27626-0531
919-733-3983

NORTH DAKOTA
Aging Services Division
Department of Human Services
P.O. Box 7070, Northbrook Shop Ctr.
N. Washington St.
Bismarck, ND 58507-7070
701-224-2577

NORTHERN MARIANA ISLANDS
Division of Veterans Affairs, DC & CA
Office of the Governors
Commonwealth of the Northern Mariana Islands
Saipan, MP 96950
Tel. 9411 or 9732

OHIO
Department of Aging
50 W. Broad St., 9th Fl.
Columbus, OH 43266-0501
614-466-5500

OKLAHOMA
Aging Services Division
Department of Human Services
P.O. Box 25352
312 NE 28th St.
Oklahoma City, OK 73125
405-521-2327

OREGON
Senior & Disabled Services Division
500 Summer St. NE, 2nd Fl. North
Salem, OR 97310
503-378-4728

PENNSYLVANIA
Department of Aging
231 State St.
Harrisburg, PA 17101-1195
717-783-1550

PUERTO RICO
Governor's Office for Elderly Affairs
Corbian Plaza Stop 23
Ponce De Leon Ave. #1603
U.M. Office C
San Ture, PR 00908
809-721-5710

RHODE ISLAND
Department of Elderly Affairs
160 Pine St.
Providence, RI 02903-3708
401-277-2858

(AMERICAN) SAMOA
Territorial Administration on Aging
American Samoa Government
Pago Pago, American Samoa 96799
011-684-633-1252

SOUTH CAROLINA
Commission on Aging
400 Arbor Lake Dr., #B-500
Columbia, SC 29223
803-735-0210

SOUTH DAKOTA
Office of Adult Services & Aging
700 Governors Dr.
Pierre, SD 57501
605-773-3656

TENNESSEE
Commission on Aging
706 Church St., Suite 201
Nashville, TN 37243-0860
615-741-2056

TEXAS
Department on Aging
P.O. Box 12786 Capitol Station
1949 IH 35, South
Austin, TX 78741-3702
512-444-2727

REPUBLIC OF PALAU
Agency on Aging
P.O. Box 100
Koror, PW 96940

UTAH
Division of Aging & Adult Services
Department of Social Services
Box 45500
120 North, 200 West
Salt Lake City, UT 84145-0500
801-538-3910

VERMONT
Aging and Disabilities
103 S. Main St.
Waterbury, VT 05676
802-241-2400

VIRGINIA
Department for the Aging
700 Centre, 10th Fl.
700 E. Franklin St.
Richmond, VA 23219-2327
804-225-2271

VIRGIN ISLANDS
Senior Citizen Affairs
Department of Human Services
#19 Estate Diamond Fredericksted
St. Croix, VI 00840
809-772-4950, ext. 46

WASHINGTON
Aging & Adult Services Administration
Department of Social & Health Services
P.O. Box 45050
Olympia, WA 98504-5050
206-586-3768

WEST VIRGINIA
Commission on Aging
Holly Grove, State Capitol
Charleston, WV 25305
304-558-3317

WISCONSIN
Bureau of Aging
Division of Community Services
217 S. Hamilton St., Suite 300
Madison, WI 53707
608-266-2536

WYOMING
Commission on Aging
Hathaway Bldg., Rm. 139
Cheyenne, WY 82002-0710
307-777-7986

APPENDIX C

Health Care
Financing Administration

The following is a list of the regional offices of the Health Care Financing Administration (HCFA).

Region I, serving Connecticut, Maine, Massachusetts, New Hampshire, Rhode Island, and Vermont.
HCFA
John F. Kennedy Federal Bldg., Rm. 2325
Boston, MA 02203
617-565-1188

Region II, serving New York, New Jersey, Puerto Rico, and the Virgin Islands.
HCFA
26 Federal Plaza, Rm. 3811
New York, NY 10278
212-264-4488

Region III, serving Delaware, Washington, DC, Maryland, Pennsylvania, Virginia, and West Virginia.
HCFA
3535 Market St., Rm. 3100
Philadelphia, PA 19101
215-596-1351

Region IV, serving Alabama, Florida, Georgia, Kentucky, Mississippi, North Carolina, South Carolina, and Tennessee.
HCFA
101 Marietta St., Suite 701
Atlanta, GA 30323
404-331-2329

Region V, serving Illinois, Indiana, Michigan, Minnesota, Ohio, and Wisconsin.
HCFA
105 West Adams St.
14th-16th Fls.
Chicago, IL 60603-6201
312-886-6432

Region VI, serving Arkansas, Louisiana, New Mexico, Oklahoma, and Texas.
HCFA
1200 Main Tower Bldg., Rm. 2000
Dallas, TX 75202
214-767-6427

Region VII, serving Iowa, Kansas, Missouri, and Nebraska.
HCFA
New Federal Office Bldg.
601 East 12th St., Rm. 235
Kansas City, MO 64106
816-426-5233

Region VIII, serving Colorado, Montana, North Dakota, South Dakota, Utah, and Wyoming.
HCFA
Federal Office Bldg.
1961 Stout St., Rm. 1185
Denver, CO 80294
303-844-2111

Region IX, serving American Samoa, Arizona, California, Guam, Hawaii, and Nevada.
HCFA
75 Hawthorne St.
4th and 5th Fls.
San Francisco, CA 94105
415-744-3502

Region X, serving Alaska, Idaho, Oregon, and Washington.
HCFA
2201 Sixth Ave.
Mail Stop RX40
Seattle, WA 98121
206-553-0425

APPENDIX D

Directory of Agencies and Organizations for Further Information

In your search for further information and assistance, don't forget to check out the services in your own locality. If you are having trouble finding help or information regarding a specific problem, you may want to contact the Eldercare Locator at 1-800-677-1116.

In addition to that, the following directory is a listing of public and private agencies that can provide further information and assistance for a variety of problems. For some of these organizations, such as the American Red Cross or the American Cancer Society, you may find a local chapter listed in your telephone book.

General Information and Assistance

American Association of Retired Persons (AARP)
601 E St., NW
Washington, DC 20049
202-434-2277

American Red Cross (National Headquarters)
430 17th St., NW
Washington, DC 20006
202-737-8300

Children of Aging Parents (CAPS)
Woodburne Campus Office, Suite 302A
1609 Woodburne Rd.
Levittown, PA 19057
215-945-6900

National Association of Area Agencies on Aging
1112 16th St., NW, Suite 100
Washington, DC 20036
202-296-8130

National Council of Senior Citizens
1331 F St., NW
Washington, DC 20004-1171
202-347-8800

National Council on the Aging, Inc.
409 3rd St., SW, Suite 200
Washington, DC 20024
202-479-1200

National Institute on Aging
(Part of the National Institutes of Health)
Public Information Center
Building 31, Rm. 5C27
9000 Rockville Pike
Bethesda, MD 20892
301-496-1752
(To order publications call 1-800-222-2225)

Regional Institute of Senior Centers
Refer to the National Council on Aging, Inc.

Superintendent of Documents
U.S. Government Printing Office
Pueblo, CO 81009

Specific Information and Assistance

Alcohol and Drug Abuse

National Clearinghouse for Alcohol and Drug
  Information
P.O. Box 2345
Rockville, MD 20847-2345
301-468-2600 (Alcohol abuse information)
301-443-6500 (Drug abuse information)

National Council on Alcoholism and Drug Abuse
12 W. 21st St.
New York, NY 10010
212-206-6770

Alzheimer's Disease and Related Disorders

Alzheimer's Disease & Related Disorders Association
919 N. Michigan Ave., Suite 1000
Chicago, IL 60611-1676
312-335-8700
1-800-272-3900
1-800-572-6037 (Illinois residents)

Alzheimer's Family Relief Program
American Health Assistance Foundation
15825 Shady Grove Rd., Suite 140
Rockville, MD 20850
1-800-437-AHAF (2423)

National Institute of Mental Health
5600 Fishers Lane, Rm. 15C-05
Rockville, MD 20892
301-443-4513

National Institute on Aging
(See address listed under "General Information and
Assistance")
1-800-438-4380 (for Alzheimer's information)

Arthritis

Arthritis Foundation
P.O. Box 19000
Atlanta, GA 30326
404-872-7100
1-800-283-7800

National Institute of Arthritis and Musculoskeletal
   and Skin Diseases Information Clearinghouse
Box AMS
9000 Rockville Pike
Bethesda, MD 20892
301-495-4484

Cancer

American Cancer Society
1599 Clifton Rd., NE
Atlanta, GA 30329-4251
404-320-3333
1-800-227-2345

National Cancer Institute
Office of Cancer Communications
Bldg. 31, Rm. 10A-24
9000 Rockville Pike
Bethesda, MD 20892
301-496-5583
1-800-4-CANCER (422-6237)

Dental Needs

American Dental Association
211 E. Chicago Ave.
Chicago, IL 60611-2678
312-440-2500

National Institute of Dental Research
Information Office
Bldg. 31, Rm. 2C-35
9000 Rockville Pike
Bethesda, MD 20892
301-496-4261

Depression and Mental Health

National Institute of Mental Health
(See information under "Alzheimer's Disease &
Related Disorders)

National Mental Health Association
1021 Prince St.
Alexandria, VA 22314-2971
703-684-7722

Diabetes

American Diabetes Association
1660 Duke St.
Alexandria, VA 22314
703-549-1500
1-800-ADA-DISC (232-3472)

National Institute of Diabetes and Digestive and
  Kidney Diseases
Information Office
Bldg. 31, Rm. 9A-04
Bethesda, MD 20892
301-496-3583

Driving Safety

American Association of Retired Persons (AARP)
(See information under "General Information and
Assistance")

American Automobile Association (AAA)
Driver Safety Services
Traffic Safety and Engineering Department
1000 AAA Dr.
Heathrow, FL 32746-5063
407-444-7961

National Safety Council
1121 Spring Lake Dr.
Itasca, IL 60143
708-285-1121
1-800-621-7619

Education

Elderhostel
75 Federal St.
Boston, MA 02110-1941
617-426-7788
617-426-8351 (fax)

Older Adult Service and Information System (OASIS)
7710 Carondelet Ave., Suite 125
St. Louis, MO 63105
314-862-2933

Employment Opportunities

American Association of Retired Persons (AARP)
(See information under "General Information and Assistance")

National Council of Senior Citizens
(See information under "General Information and
Assistance")

National Council on the Aging, Inc.
(See information under "General Information and
Assistance")

National Displaced Homemakers Network
1625 K St. NW, Suite 300
Washington, DC 20006
202-467-6346

Older Adult Service and Information System (OASIS)
(See information under "Education")

Eyes

American Council of the Blind
1155 15th St. NW, Suite 720
Washington, DC 20005
202-467-5081
1-800-424-8666

American Foundation for the Blind
15 W. 16th St.
New York, NY 10011
212-620-2000
1-800-232-5463

American Optometric Association
243 N. Lindbergh Blvd.
St. Louis, MO 63141
314-991-4100

Foundation for Glaucoma Research
490 Post St., Suite 830
San Francisco, CA 94102
415-986-3162

The Lighthouse National Center for Vision and
    Aging
800 2nd Ave.
New York, NY 10017
212-808-0077
1-800-334-5497

National Eye Institute
Information Office
Building 31, Rm. 6A-32
9000 Rockville Pike
Bethesda, MD 20892
301-496-5248

National Society to Prevent Blindness
500 E. Remington Rd.
Schaumberg, IL 60173
708-843-2020
1-800-331-2020

Geriatric Care (Case) Managers

National Association of Private Geriatric Care
  Managers
655 N. Alvernon Way, Suite 108
Tucson, AZ 85711
602-881-8008

Hearing

American Speech-Language-Hearing Association
10801 Rockville Pike
Rockville, MD 20852
301-897-5700
1-800-638-8255
1-800-897-8682 (for Maryland residents)

National Information Center on Deafness
Gallaudet University
800 Florida Ave., NE
Washington, DC 20002-3695
202-651-5051

National Institute on Deafness and Other
  Communication Disorders
Building 31, Rm. 3C-35
9000 Rockville Pike
Bethesda, MD 20892
301-496-7243

Self Help for Hard of Hearing People
7800 Wisconsin Ave.
Bethesda, MD 20814
301-657-2248

Heart Disease

American Heart Association
7272 Greenville Ave.
Dallas, TX 75231
214-373-6300
(Check your local phone book for a toll-free number
serving your state.)

National Heart, Lung and Blood Information Center
P.O. Box 30105
Bethesda, MD 20824-0105
301-951-3260

Home Health Care

National Association of Home Care
519 C St., NE
Washington, DC 20002
202-547-7424

National Hospice Organization
1901 N. Moore St., Suite 901
Arlington, VA 22209
1-800-658-8898

Incontinence

Help for Incontinent People (HIP)
P.O. Box 544
Union, SC 29379
803-579-7900

The Simon Foundation
P.O. Box 835-F
Wilmette, IL 60091
708-864-3913
1-800-23-SIMON (237-4666)

Insurance

For information about insurance, contact state office on aging (listed in a separate appendix in this book) or your state department of insurance. Or contact the agency listed below.

Health Insurance Association of America
Consumer Information Service
1025 Connecticut Ave., NW
Washington, DC 20036
202-223-7788
1-800-942-4242 (Hotline)

Kidney Disease

National Institute of Diabetes and Digestive and
   Kidney Disease
(See information under "Diabetes")

National Kidney Foundation, Inc.
30 E. 33rd St.
New York, NY 10016
212-889-2210
1-800-622-9010

Lung and Respiratory Disease

American Lung Association
1740 Broadway
New York, NY 10019
212-315-8700

National Heart, Lung and Blood Information Center
(See information under "Heart Disease")

National Jewish Center for Immunology and
    Respiratory Medicine
1400 Jackson St.
Denver, CO 80206
303-388-1644
1-800-222-5864

Medic Alert

Medic Alert Foundation
P.O. Box 1009
Turlock, CA 95381
209-668-3333
1-800-344-3226

Nutrition

American Dietetic Association
216 W. Jackson Blvd., Suite 800
Chicago, IL 60606-6995
312-899-0040
1-800-877-1600

Ombudsman

To find the ombudsman nearest to you, check your local phone book or contact your state department on aging (listed in Appendix B in this book), your local Area Agency on Aging, or the Eldercare Locator (call 1-800-677-1116).

Osteoporosis

National Institute of Arthritis and Musculoskeletal
  and Skin Diseases
(See information under "Arthritis")

National Osteoporosis Foundation
1150 17th St. NW, Suite 500
Washington, DC 20036
202-223-2226
1-800-223-9994

Recreation, Sports, and Fitness

National Recreation and Park Association
2775 S. Quincy St., Suite 300
Alexandria, VA 22206
703-820-4940

National Senior Sports Association
1248 Post Rd.
Fairfield, CN 06430
203-254-2656
1-800-282-NSSA (6772)

U.S. National Senior Sports Organization
14323 S. Outer 40 Rd., Suite N300
Chesterfield, MO 63017
314-878-4900

Rehabilitation

National Rehabilitation Information Center
8455 Colesville Rd., Suite 935
Silver Spring, MD 20910-3319
301-588-9284
1-800-346-2742

Social Security and Medicare

Social Security Administration
Baltimore, MD 21235
1-800-772-1213

Strokes

National Institute of Neurological Disorders and
    Stroke Information Office
Bldg. 31, Rm. 8A-16
9000 Rockville Pike
Bethesda, MD 20892
301-496-5751

National Stroke Association
8480 E. Orchard Rd., Suite 1000
Englewood, CO 80111-5015
303-762-9922
1-800-STROKES (787-6537)

Support Groups

American Self-Help Clearinghouse
St. Clairs Riverside Medical Center
25 Pocono Rd.
Denville, NJ 07834
201-625-7101

Veterans' Benefits

U.S. Department of Veterans Affairs
Office of Public Affairs
810 Vermont Ave., NW
Washington, DC 20420
1-800-827-1000
For specific information call the numbers listed
  below:
  Life Insurance: 1-800-669-8477
  Radiation Helpline: 1-800-827-0365
  Debt Management: 1-800-827-0648
  Education Loan: 1-800-326-8276
  CHAMPVA: 1-800-733-8387
  Telecommunications for the Deaf (TDD): 1-800-
829-4833

Women's Health Issues

American College of Obstetricians & Gynecologists
409 12th St., SW
Washington, DC 20024
202-638-5577
1-800-673-8444

For additional names and addresses of agencies that serve senior citizens, contact the National Institute on Aging and ask for the *Resource Directory on Older People.*

APPENDIX E

Legal Resources

If you need to locate free or low-cost legal assistance in your area, contact your local Area Agency on Aging or Human Services Information Center for advice and information. In addition to those agencies, the following list suggests some resources that offer aid in legal issues such as estate planning and in cases of elder abuse. Some of these organizations, like the Federal Trade Commission, have state offices that provide more specific information and help.

National Senior Citizens Law Center
1815 H St. NW
Washington, DC 20006
202-887-5280

Legal Counsel for the Elderly
601 E St., NW
Washington, DC 20049
202-434-2120

House Select Committee on Aging
712 O'Neill Bldg.
300 New Jersey Ave., SE
Washington, DC 20515
202-226-3375
(This committee examines legal programs for and delivery of legal services to the elderly.)

Federal Trade Commission
6th St. and Pennsylvania Ave., NW
Washington, DC 20580
To locate an office near you, call 202-326-2000
For general information, call 202-326-2180

National Research and Information Center
2250 E. Devon, Suite 250
Des Plaines, IL 60018
1-800-662-7666
(This organization arbitrates consumer complaints involving funeral directors.)

Equal Employment Opportunity Commission
1-800-669-4000
(If you feel you have been discriminated against in employment because of your age, you can file a charge with your local EEOC. Since this is a beleaguered office, action may be slow. For locations and more information, call the toll-free number above.)

National Coalition Against Domestic Violence
P.O. Box 34103
Washington, DC 20043
202-638-6388

National Organization for Victim Assistance
1757 Park Road, NW
Washington, DC 20010
202-232-6682

National Academy of Elder Law Attorneys
655 N. Elvernon Way, Suite 108
Tucson, AZ 85711
602-881-4005
(This organization lists elder law attorneys by state and provides a brochure of other legal reference information.)

Appendix F

Small Business Administration Services and Directory

The U.S. Small Business Administration (SBA) offers a variety of services for those who need help or information to start or maintain a small business.

For instance, the SBA **Office of Business Development** works to develop and maintain a statewide network of management training, counseling, and technical assistance programs. Videotapes and publications addressing financial management, management and planning, crime prevention, marketing, personnel management, and products/ideas/inventions, are all available through the SBA.

The Service Corps of Retired Executives (SCORE) is an independent, nonprofit organization of retired business persons who volunteer their time to provide free counseling and low-cost training to small business owners and prospective entrepreneurs.

Through workshops and one-on-one counseling, SCORE provides the beginning entrepreneur with a solid base of knowledge to launch a new business venture. Existing business owners also can benefit from the experience of retired business owners who have operated successful enterprises. You may want to volunteer for SCORE, or you may want to enlist their services.

Small Business Institutes allow SBA to contract long-term consulting services from colleges and universities to provide in-depth consulting and technical assistance to small businesses free of charge. A team of students works with the client, under the guidance of a faculty coordinator, for one semester. Case assignments are coordinated with the beginning of semesters, in August and January.

The SBA also offers a network of **Small Business Development Centers**. They provide in-depth management training, counseling, and technical assistance to existing or aspiring entrepreneurs.

In addition, the SBA offers certain loan opportunities as well as special assistance programs for minority businesses, women's business ownership, international trade, etc.

For additional information about these and other services offered by the U.S. Small Business Administration, I encourage you to contact the national offices at 409 Third Street SW, Washington, DC 20416, or call 202-205-7000. Or perhaps you would prefer to contact one of the following regional offices.

Region I, serving Connecticut, Maine, Massachusetts, New Hampshire, Rhode Island, and Vermont.
Boston Regional Office
155 Federal St., 9th Fl.
Boston, MA 02110
617-451-2023
617-565-8695 (fax)
617-451-0491 (TDD)

Region II, serving New Jersey, New York, Puerto Rico, and the Virgin Islands.
New York Regional Office
26 Federal Plaza, Rm. 31-08
New York, NY 10278
212-264-1450
212-264-0900 (fax)
212-264-5669 (TDD)

Region III, serving Delaware, Maryland, Pennsylvania, Virginia, West Virginia, and Washington, DC.
Philadelphia Regional Office
Allendale Square, Suite 201
475 Allendale Rd.
King of Prussia, PA 19406
215-962-3700
215-962-3743 (fax)
215-962-3739 (TDD)

Region IV, serving Kentucky, Tennessee, North Carolina, South Carolina, Mississippi, Alabama, Georgia, and Florida.

    Atlanta Regional Office
    1375 Peachtree Street, NE, 5th Fl.
    Atlanta, GA 30367-8102
    404-347-2797
    404-347-2355 (fax)
    404-347-5051 (TDD)

Region V, serving Minnesota, Wisconsin, Michigan, Illinois, Indiana, and Ohio.

    Chicago Regional Office
    300 South Riverside Plaza, Rm. 1975 S.
    Chicago, IL 60606-6607
    312-353-5000
    312-353-3426 (fax)
    312-353-8060 (TDD)

Region VI, serving New Mexico, Oklahoma, Arkansas, Texas, and Louisiana.

    Dallas Regional Office
    8625 King George Dr., Bldg. C
    Dallas, TX 75235-3391
    214-767-7635
    214-767-7870 (fax)
    214-767-1339 (TDD)

Region VII, serving Iowa, Missouri, Nebraska, and Kansas.

Kansas City Regional Office
911 Walnut St., 13th Fl.
Kansas City, MO 64106
816-426-3608
816-426-5559 (fax)
816-426-2990 (TDD)

Region VIII, serving Montana, North Dakota, South Dakota, Wyoming, Utah, and Colorado.

Denver Regional Office
Denver Place
999 18th St., Suite 701
Denver, CO 80202
303-294-7186
303-294-7153 (fax)
303-294-7096 (TDD)

Region IX, serving California, Nevada, Arizona, Hawaii, and Guam.

San Francisco Regional Office
71 Stevenson St., 20th Fl.
San Francisco, CA 94105-2939
415-744-6402
415-744-6435 (fax)
415-744-6401 (TDD)

Region X, serving Washington, Oregon, Idaho, and Alaska.
   Seattle Regional Office
   Fourth & Vine Bldg., Rm. 440
   2615 Fourth Ave.
   Seattle, WA 98121
   206-553-5676
   206-553-4155 (fax)

APPENDIX G

Nutrition
Made Easier

When you choose a new diet, be sure to select one you can stick with easily. Even the best plan won't help if you tuck it in a drawer after only a week or two.

Rather than depriving yourself of all the foods you enjoy, I recommend that you simply replace your high-calorie, high-fat dishes with tasty, healthful foods. Try the good nutrition recipes you find in magazines and cookbooks. Eating "better" can mean eating better tasting food, and it will improve your health.

On Cookbooks

You will find it helpful to look for cookbooks specifically geared toward better eating. Countless cookbooks today cater to the nutritional needs of people over fifty. I've even seen cookbooks for seniors living alone who aren't used to fixing smaller portions. Find a cookbook you can trust, such as one put together by a team of dietitians or gerontologists. If you're not sure you want to invest in these specialized cookbooks, go to your public library. You will find a wide range of specialized cookbooks that you can use for free.

Elements of Nutrition

Most likely you have at least a vague understanding of the division of food groups. You remember that it is important to eat a balanced diet with a certain number of portions from each category. With diet fads and diet specialists telling us what to avoid and what to keep track of, the basic food groups and their important elements sometimes get muddled. Here are some basics on the elements of nutrition.

Nutrients

Our bodies need nutrients to provide energy, to grow and repair living tissue, and to regulate certain body functions. Nutrients fall into two major categories —macronutrients and micronutrients—and each of those categories has three sub-categories. Macronutrients are carbohydrates, fats, and proteins. Micronutrients are vitamins, minerals, and water.

Macronutrients

Carbohydrates. Carbohydrates, which are manufactured by green plants, have one primary purpose—to provide energy to our bodies. Starches, also called complex carbohydrates, are found in grains, cereals, legumes, potatoes, and other vegetables. Sugars, or simple carbohydrates, are found mainly in fruit and milk. These foods are also good sources of vitamins, minerals, fiber, and calories. Be aware of your intake of high–calorie favorites like sweet desserts, candy, honey, syrup, and other sugary foods. Since they provide few nutrients other than sugar, they have a lot of empty calories. And remember, breads and cereals are more nutritious when made from whole grains.

Fats. Fats provide a concentrated source of energy, because they are high in calories. You need some fat in your diet to allow your body to use fat-soluble vitamins A, D, E, and K. Fat also gives flavor to food. However, according to the National Institute of Health, American diets tend to include too much fat. Therefore, major fat sources such as eggs and organ meat should be limited, as should butter, cream, mayonnaise, margarine oils, lard, salad dressings, gravies, sauces, certain prepared foods, and snack foods such as potato chips. A healthful diet will emphasize low-fat foods such as fish, poultry, lean meat, dry beans and peas, skim milk, yogurt, buttermilk, fruit, vegetables, and grains. The quantity of fat actually required by the body is extremely small, and overconsumption of fats automatically increases your calorie intake. Whereas fat contains nine calories per gram, proteins and carbohydrates each contain only four calories per gram. As you can see, this means that equal amounts of fat versus protein or carbohydrates have very different effects on the body.

Protein. Considered to be the building material of the body, protein enables the body to repair and replace its cells and to form antibodies that resist disease. The millions of different kinds of protein are all made of twenty different components called amino acids. Once the body breaks the proteins into these amino acids, it reassembles them into new compounds. The body then uses them to build and maintain its own structural composition or to perform the various functions I mentioned previously.

The most common sources of protein are meat, fish, dairy products, and eggs, which contain all eight essential amino acids in proper amounts for adults. Plant foods such as dry peas and beans, grains, nuts, and seeds contain "incomplete" proteins because not all of the essential amino acids are present. However, when one of these incomplete sources is combined with an animal protein (milk with cereal, for example) or when certain plant proteins are combined (such as rice with beans), they form complete proteins.

The Micronutrients

Water. Although it often is overlooked in nutrition plans, water really is the essential component of our diets. The human body is actually two-thirds water. Your body can survive longer without food than it can without water.

Vitamins. As the organic chemicals essential to human life, vitamins perform different functions in the body. A lack of any one of them can cause deficiency diseases such as scurvy or rickets. Yet, vitamins are needed by the body in relatively small amounts. Fat-soluble vitamins A, D, E, and K are absorbed from various foods and are stored in the body. Water-soluble vitamins, the Bs and C, generally are not stored.

Minerals. Like vitamins, minerals are needed only in small amounts. Their effect is only dimly understood. Too much of a mineral is as potentially dangerous as too little. It is known that minerals such as calcium, phosphorus, iron, iodine, magnesium, and zinc also are required to build body tissues and regulate their functions.

Older people should pay particular attention to their need for calcium. Women past menopause may develop a disorder called osteoporosis, which makes the bones fragile and brittle and often leads to painful and disabling fractures. You can help your body avoid a calcium shortage by including in your daily diet foods that are high in calcium, such as milk, yogurt, and cheese.

The Food Groups

By organizing foods into categories or food groups and by eating the recommended number of servings from each category, we can ensure a healthful diet that provides the nutrients we need. On the following pages I provide a guide to a well-balanced diet. Called the New American Eating Guide, it was put together by the Center for Science in the Public Interest. It is based on widely accepted nutritional principles of preventive medicine.

In the guide, commonly eaten foods are organized

into categories of relatively valuable and less-valuable foods, making it easy for you to balance your diet. The "anytime" foods should be the backbone of your diet. They are low in fat, sugar, and salt. Grain foods are mostly unrefined whole grains; therefore, they are high in fiber and trace minerals.

The "in moderation" foods contain moderate amounts of either saturated fats (which usually come from animals and are our primary dietary source of cholesterol), or unsaturated fats (which usually come from plants and do not contain cholesterol). While some items contain large amounts of fat, most of these are monounsaturated or polyunsaturated. In general, polyunsaturated fats contain no cholesterol. Monounsaturated fats also contain no cholesterol, and they may even work to lower cholesterol levels within the body. Footnotes in the table indicate the drawbacks of the foods listed.

The "now and then" foods should be eaten in smaller portions and eaten less often than other foods. They are usually high in fat, with large amounts of saturated fats, or they are very high in sugar, salt, or cholesterol.

The important thing to keep in mind with a guide like this is that no single food supplies all the nutrients you need. There is no perfect combination of foods that will ensure your health and well-being. But if you eat a variety of foods in a well-balanced plan, you'll usually get all the nutrients you need, and you will be modifying risks.

GROUP 1. BEANS, GRAINS, AND NUTS
(four or more servings per day)

Any Time	In Moderation	Now and Then
bread and rolls (whole grain)	Cornbread[8] flour tortilla[8] granola cereal[1 or 2] hominy grits[8] macaroni and cheese[1,(6),8] matzoh[8] nuts[3] pasta (other than whole wheat)[8] peanut butter[3] refined, unsweetened cereals[8] refried beans, commercial or homemade in oil[2] seeds[3] soybeans[2] tofu[2] waffles or pancakes with syrup[5,(6),8] white bread and rolls[8] white rice[8]	croissant[4,8] Doughnut (yeast-leavened)[3 or 4,5,8] presweetened breakfast cereals[5,8] sticky buns[1 or 2,5,8] stuffing (made with butter)[4,(6),8]

GROUP 2. FRUITS AND VEGETABLES
(four or more servings per day)

Any Time	In Moderation	Now and Then
All fruits and vegetables except those listed at right applesauce (unsweetened) unsweetened fruit juices unsalted vegetable juices potatoes, white or sweet	avocado[3] cole slaw[3] cranberry sauce (canned)[5] dried fruit french fries, home-made in vegetable oil[2] or commercial[1] fried eggplant (vegetable oil)[2] fruits canned in syrup[5] gazpacho[2,(6)] guacamole[3] potatoes au gratin[1,(6)] salted vegetable juices[6] sweetened fruit juices[5] vegetables canned with salt[6]	coconut[4] pickles[6]

GROUP 3. MILK PRODUCTS
(children: three to four servings per day;
adults: two servings per day)

Any Time	In Moderation	Now and Then
buttermilk made from skim milk	cocoa made with skim milk[5]	cheesecake[4,5] cheese fondue[4,(6)]

lassi (lowfat yogurt and fruit juice drink)
lowfat cottage cheese
lowfat milk, one percent milkfat
lowfat yogurt
nonfat dry milk
skim milk
skim milk cheeses
skim milk and banana shake

cottage cheese, regular, 4 percent milkfat[1]
frozen lowfat yogurt[5]
lowfat milk, 2 percent milkfat[1]
lowfat yogurt, unsweetened[5]
mozzarella cheese, part-skim type only[1,(6)]

cheese soufflé[4,(6),7]
eggnog[1,5,7]
hard cheese: bleu, brick, Camembert, cheddar, Muenster, Swiss[4,(6)]
ice cream[4,5]
processed cheeses[4,6]
whole milk[4]
whole milk yogurt[4]

GROUP 4. POULTRY, FISH, MEAT AND EGGS
(two servings per day)

Any Time	In Moderation	Now and Then
Poultry: chicken, or turkey, boiled, baked or roasted (no skin)	**Poultry:** chicken liver, baked or broiled[7] (just one) fried chicken, homemade in vegetable oil[3] chicken or turkey, boiled, baked, or roasted (with skin)[2]	**Poultry:** fried chicken, commercially prepared[4]
Fish: cod flounder gefilte fish[6] haddock halibut perch pollack rockfish shellfish other than shrimp sole tuna, water-packed[(6)]	**Fish:** (drained well, if canned) fried fish[1 or 2] herring[3,6] mackerel, canned[2,(6)] salmon, pink, canned[2,(6)] sardines[2] shrimp[7] tuna, oil-packed[2,(6)]	

Red Meats (trimmed of all outside fat):	**Red meats:**
leg or loin of lamb[1]	bacon[4,(6)]
pork shoulder or loin, lean[1]	beef liver, fried[1,7]
	bologna[4,6]
round steak or ground round[1]	corned beef[4,6]
	ground beef[4,6]
rump roast[1]	ham, trimmed well[1,6]
sirloin steak, lean[1]	hot dogs[4,6]
veal[1]	liverwurst[4,6]
	pig's feet[4]
	salami[4,6]
	sausage[4,6]
	spareribs[4]
	untrimmed red meats[4]
Egg Products:	**Eggs:**
egg whites only	cheese omelet[4,7]
	egg yolk or whole egg (about three per week)[3,7]

Source: Center for Science in the Public Interest
Notes: The small numbers after items in the chart denote a food's drawbacks.

[1]moderate fat, saturated
[2]moderate fat, unsaturated
[3]high fat, unsaturated
[4]high fat, saturated
[5]high in added sugar
[6]high in salt or sodium
[(6)]may be high in salt or sodium, depending on manufacturer or recipe
[7]high in cholesterol
[8]refined grains

Dietary Goals

Because changing your diet is never as easy as it sounds, it is important to establish specific goals. The following list of goals also explains the kind of change they will require, and their potential overall benefits.

Goal 1

To avoid gaining weight, consume only as much energy (calories) as you expend. Individual caloric needs vary from person to person, depending on age, sex, body type and activity level. As we get older, our metabolism slows down. That means we need less energy—fewer calories—to fuel our bodies and maintain an ideal weight. For this reason, it is more important than ever to supply our bodies with foods of high nutritional value and to avoid foods of little or no nutritional worth.

Therefore, if you are overweight, decrease your calorie intake and increase your energy expenditure. Controlling the size of your food portions is one of the most effective ways to monitor your calorie intake. Plus, eating smaller portions allows you to continue to enjoy a wide variety of foods.

There is far more to being overweight than not fitting society's notions of physical attractiveness. Being overweight threatens your life. Overweight individuals are more likely to suffer from heart disease, atherosclerosis, hernia, thyroid disease, colitis, ulcer, and cancer. You owe it to yourself and those you love to try to stay alive and healthy by slimming down.

Goal 2

Increase your consumption of complex carbohydrates and "naturally occurring" sugars from about 28 percent to about 48 percent of calorie intake. As I noted previously, you will find complex carbohydrates in grains, starches, legumes, and vegetables. Naturally occurring sugars come in fruit and milk. Carbohydrates should supply at least half of your daily calories. To achieve this goal, cut down on refined and processed sugars such as table sugar and corn syrup. These simple carbohydrates are higher in calories and lower in overall nutritional value.

Natural carbohydrates also provide fiber. While fiber is not the magic ingredient many have presented it to be, we need natural fiber to keep the food we eat moving through our digestive system. Lack of fiber has been strongly linked to cancer of the colon and diverticulitis, an inflammation of small pockets that develop in the lower bowel. You can boost your dietary fiber to the recommended 20 to 30 grams a day by eating unpeeled fresh fruit and vegetables; eating boiled or baked potatoes with the skin; eating whole grain breads; using oats, oatmeal, cracked wheat, and barley; eating cooked peas and beans often; eating popcorn; substituting one half or all whole wheat flour in recipes calling for white flour; and choosing brown rice instead of white rice. Overall, just eat more fruits, vegetables, and whole grain foods.

Complex carbohydrates benefit weight control and

help balance your food budget. You can buy the finest fruits and vegetables on the market and still not spend what you would on steak. By concentrating on complex carbohydrate foods, you will have no trouble controlling your weight, as long as you stick with relatively unsweetened baked goods, eat vegetables and fruits, and avoid large helpings of heavy sauces on your pasta and rice.

Goal 3

Reduce your overall fat consumption to about 30 percent of calorie intake. Remember, fat contains about nine calories per gram compared to the four calories per gram in protein and carbohydrates.

Goal 4

Reduce saturated fat consumption to account for about 10 percent of total calorie intake; and balance that with polyunsaturated and monounsaturated fats, which should account for about 10 percent of calorie intake each. To determine what your total intake of fat should be, divide the number of calories for the day by 30. For example, if you eat 1,800 calories a day, your fat intake should be 60 grams.

Next, identify the high-fat foods you eat and how much of them you eat. Try to make healthy substitutions as you gradually cut back on your portions of this food. The amount of fat can be cut in half just by paying attention to the amounts you consume. Skip high-fat foods entirely if you can. Simply cutting back on salad dressings and margarines, or substituting naturally sweetened fruit spreads for butter on toast can make a difference.

Goal 5

Reduce cholesterol consumption to about 300 milligrams a day.

Goals 3, 4, and 5 are based on the assumption that excess cholesterol in the bloodstream can cause heart disease and other related diseases. Obviously it is desirable to lower the levels of fat and cholesterol in the blood, and this may be accomplished in part through diet.

Because the dietary guidelines suggest a daily maximum of 300 milligrams of cholesterol, you should eat shellfish, liver, and eggs in moderation. Each egg, for example, contains 250 milligrams. Now consider the amount of cholesterol in other foods you consume throughout the day.

The best course is to cut back on the total fat in your diet. Use lowfat cooking oils, particularly those with polyunsaturated fats, and lowfat cooking methods such as broiling, steaming, and baking rather than frying.

Goal 6

Reduce sodium by reducing the intake of salt to about five grams a day. Salt, like fat, imparts a lot of the flavor in food that we have become used to over the years. Although sodium is an essential mineral, too much sodium in your diet may lead to high blood pressure, or hypertension. Scientists have shown that sodium intake raises the blood pressure of some hypertensive individuals and may actually cause hypertension in certain individuals. The substance won't cause the disease unless you have a hereditary weakness, but in large amounts it appears to bring on the disease if the tendency is present in your genetic makeup.

More than 10 million Americans are known to suffer from high blood pressure, and an unknown number of additional cases remain undiagnosed. This all points to one suggestion: *Cut back on your salt intake.*

You can cut back on your intake of salt and other chemical additives simply by turning to fresh foods. Use fresh or frozen vegetables rather than canned. The difference in sodium content may be as much as 300 milligrams. Use spices and herbs to replace the flavor of salt. For example, if a recipe calls for garlic salt, use fresh garlic or garlic powder. Cut back on processed and cured meats like hot dogs and cold cuts. Look for food labeled "sodium free" (about 5 milligrams of sodium), "very low sodium" (less than 35 milligrams) and "low sodium" (140 milligrams).

New FDA regulations require food companies to label their products so you can clearly read how much sodium, fat, and cholesterol is in each product. At the same time, more and more companies are producing health-conscious products. All of this makes it easier for you to keep track of the types of food you're eating and to maintain a healthy diet.

APPENDIX H

Fitness
Is for You

Like good nutrition, exercise will have a positive effect on your life. In fact, the impact will be far reaching.

Jane Brody, health columnist for the *New York Times,* writes, "Exercise can help your heart become a more efficient pump, increase your stamina, enhance your ability to deliver oxygen to your muscles and clear away waste products, keep your coronary arteries and other arteries wide open, lower your blood pressure, normalize your blood sugar, strengthen your bones with added calcium, increase the flexibility in your joints, slow the loss of lean muscle tissue and deter the accumulation of body fat." She also points out that exercise can enhance your mental sharpness and emotional stability and even improve the quality of sleep.[1]

With all of these possibilities, it is clear that the earlier you start exercising, the better off you will be. If you are in reasonably good health, a brisk walk will make your blood flow faster, put some fresh air in your lungs, and generally increase your alertness. The exhilaration of sharpened senses will inspire your continued efforts toward physical fitness.

A recent study at the USDA Human Nutrition Research Center on Aging at Tufts University concluded that people over 45 who continue to be physically active have a much better chance of maintaining vigor, stamina, and physical flexibility as well as overall health. The researchers say: "Even if you're already 75 years old, feel overburdened with aches and pains, and have long since accepted the idea that an energetic lifestyle is over for you, you can still turn things around."

The benefits of exercise are not limited to a renewed sense of youthfulness and energy. Studies by the National Institute on Aging found that exercise is as effective as, and sometimes more effective, than medication.

This was particularly true in two studies on urinary incontinence. One study involved a six-week program of bladder training. Of the 123 women over 55 years of age, 12 percent became continent again, while three quarters of them improved 50 percent or more. The second study actually compared the use of pelvic muscle exercise to drug treatment. The results showed that the nondrug treatment was at least as successful as the drug treatment. This success is especially significant for elders, many of whom take multiple medications. Finding a nondrug treatment offers an alternative that may decrease one's total number of medications, and thus also decrease the risk of adverse side effects from mixing various drugs.

As you can see, the benefits of exercise may impact your entire sense of well-being. That's a lot to look forward to. I encourage you to meet with your doctor to select a fitness plan that will work for you.

Your Exercise Program

To be effective, exercise must become a regular part of your life. You will not be able to stick with a program that conflicts with your personality, your lifestyle, and your abilities. Your physical fitness program will have three goals:

1. *Cardio-respiratory fitness.* Maintenance and improvement of your circulatory system and lung capacity is the key to lowering your chances of heart disease.

2. *Flexibility.* When you are able to move smoothly and easily through exercise, your everyday movements will seem easier and you can fight the feeling of "creakiness" or stiffness.

3. *Strength.* Increasing your muscular strength gives you power to move and carry things yourself, to be self-sufficient, and to maintain an attractive appearance.

Avoid exercises you despise. Also, avoid exercises that lock your joints in place, such as push-ups. Exercises like sit-ups and toe-touching are bad for stiff knees and your back, and they do little to build muscles. Forget about them too.

Your exercise program should focus on movement.

The only kinds of exercise that will build heart and lung capacity are aerobic exercises. Popularized by Kenneth Cooper, these activities force your body to use more oxygen, to breathe more heavily, and increase your pulse rate for a prolonged period. Aerobic exercises include walking, running, jogging, rope skipping, swimming, bicycling, skating, rowing, cross-country skiing, and aerobic dance. Any of these, combined with simple stretching movements, can get you into excellent physical shape.

You also can get more exercise into your day by making some simple choices. Take a look at your daily schedule. How can you make your day a little more active? For example, climb the stairs even when you don't have to. With every step you take upward, you lift your entire body a few inches, strengthening your legs and your cardiovascular system. Soon you'll find that with just a few minutes of exercise like this, you've done yourself some good.

Fitness Plan of Action

As I mentioned, your exercise goal is movement. You want to increase your heart rate and breathing. To determine your target heart rate, start by subtracting your age from 220. The result is your maximum heart rate. Your target heart rate is between 70 and 85 percent of your maximum heart rate. The following chart will give you some idea of your target heart rate based on the number of beats per 10 seconds.

Age	60% of maximum heart rate	75% of maximum heart rate	85% of maximum heart rate	Maximum heart rate, 100%
55	16.5 beats per 10 secs.	20.6 beats per 10 secs.	23.3 beats per 10 secs.	27.5 beats per 10 secs.
60	16 beats per 10 secs.	20 beats per 10 secs.	22.7 beats per 10 secs.	26.7 beats per 10 secs.
65	15.5 beats per 10 secs.	19.3 beats per 10 secs.	21.9 beats per 10 secs.	25.8 beats per 10 secs.
70	15 beats per 10 secs.	18.7 beats per 10 secs.	21.2 beats per 10 secs.	25 beats per 10 secs.
75	14.4 beats per 10 secs.	18 beats per 10 secs.	20.5 beats per 10 secs.	24 beats per 10 secs.
80	13.8 beats per 10 secs.	17.2 beats per 10 secs.	19.5 beats per 10 secs.	23 beats per 10 secs.

Keep in mind that you should discuss any exercise regimen with your doctor before you begin. Start slowly. There should be no pain involved in exercising. The saying "no pain, no gain" is simplistic and misleading. Different people have different pain thresholds, and while some discomfort may be encountered with effective exercise, real pain can indicate you are injuring yourself.

If you intend to increase your level of physical activity in a way that will make large and sudden demands on your circulatory system, consult your doctor again.

Exercises

Following are exercises recommended by medical professors at the UCLA Center on Aging. These exercises are specifically designed for those confined to a wheelchair or who have stability problems. The only piece of exercise equipment you need is a chair.

Deep Breathing

Sit up straight with your lower back pressed firmly against the chair. Hold your head up. Put your hands on your hips. Inhale deeply through your nose, and hold your breath while you count to three. Exhale by blowing slowly and gently through your lips as though you were whistling. Repeat three times.

Yawn and Stretch

Take a huge yawn, and slowly stretch your arms out to the sides and down. Repeat three times.

Relax Your Neck

Turn your head slowly to the right, pause for a count of two. Now turn it slowly to the left, pause. Look slowly up to the ceiling, and pause again. Repeat two times.

Apple Picker

One at a time, raise each arm overhead, and then lower it to your side. Inhale as you raise your arm, and exhale as you lower it. Repeat with each arm three times.

Squeeze Those Fingers

Stretch your arms straight out in front of you with the palms down. Squeeze your fingers slowly, then release them. Repeat five times.

Now turn your palms up and squeeze your fingers five more times. Then turn your palms down again and shake your hands five times.

Roll Your Shoulders

With your arms loosely at your sides (or with hands placed on shoulders), slowly roll your shoulders forward in circles and repeat five times. Now reverse the motion. Roll your shoulders backward in full circles and repeat five times. Move slowly. Now shrug your shoulders and relax them five times.

Loosen Your Wrists

Grasp your right hand with your left hand. Keeping your right palm facing down, rotate your right hand slowly, five times one way, and five times back the other way. Now switch hands, and rotate your left hand slowly, five times each way. You should feel your joints loosening up.

Side Stretch

Place your left hand on your left hip. Stretch your right arm over your head, and then bend toward your left side while you count to two. Move gently and smoothly; do not bounce. Return to straight up.

Now place your right hand on your right hip, extend your other arm over your head, and bend smoothly toward the right side while you count to two. Return to straight up. Repeat the movement on each side three times.

Relax Your Lower Back

Sit up straight. Bend straight forward slowly, and then straighten up. Clasp your hands on your left knee, and slowly bend toward your hands. Straighten up.

Now clasp your hands on your right knee, and slowly bend toward your hands. Straighten up. Repeat each movement three times.

Leg Extensions

Lift one leg off the floor, and stretch it out straight ahead, up to chair height if you can. Lower it slowly. Now lift the other leg off the floor and stretch it straight out. Lower it slowly. Repeat the movement with each leg five times.

Loosen Your Feet and Ankles

Cross one leg over your other knee, and rotate the foot slowly. Do ten rotations. Now cross the other leg, and rotate the other foot. Repeat ten times. Eventually, try to rotate each foot both clockwise and counterclockwise ten times.

With your legs crossed, flex each foot backward and forward. Clench your toes and release. Repeat five times for each foot.

Walking Program for Aerobic Conditioning

The following table shows a thirty-minute walking program designed for those who are in fairly poor condition. This regimen, developed by YMCA fitness experts, uses two walking paces—a stroll (covering a mile in about eighteen minutes, this is a fairly relaxed walk) and a brisk walk (covering a mile in about thirteen minutes). Of course, you are free to adjust the pace to fit the way you feel and the way your heart rate reacts. Doctors have found that one of the best exercises for overall fitness is walking. It is easier on your joints, and you still enjoy the benefits of a serious workout.

This program is broken up into two halves, the first somewhat more strenuous than the second. After the first fifteen-minute segment, take your pulse and make sure that you are on target. If not, increase or decrease your activity accordingly.

Walking Program
for Aerobic Conditioning

	First 15 Minutes	**Second 15 Minutes**
Week 1 Week 2	30 minutes of continuous	strolling
Week 3	stroll 3 minutes, brisk walk 1 minute (repeat until 15 minutes expire)	stroll 5 minutes, brisk walk 1 minute (repeat until 15 minutes expire)
Week 4	stroll 2 minutes, brisk walk 2 minutes	stroll 4 minutes, brisk walk 2 minutes

Week 5	stroll 2 minutes, brisk walk 3 minutes	stroll 4 minutes, brisk walk 3 minutes
Week 6	stroll 1 minute, brisk walk 4 minutes	stroll 3 minutes, brisk walk 4 minutes
Week 7	stroll 1 minute, brisk walk 5 minutes	stroll 2 minutes, brisk walk 5 minutes
Week 8	stroll 1 minute, brisk walk 6 minutes	stroll 2 minutes, brisk walk 6 minutes
Week 9	stroll 1 minute, brisk walk 7 minutes	stroll 1 minute, brisk walk 7 minutes
Week 10	full 15 minutes brisk walking	full 15 minutes varied-pace walking

Exercise Programs

If exercising under supervision or in a group fits into your routine more suitably, look into fitness programs available in your area. Most communities have centers where older people can join exercise classes. Check out the local church or synagogue, civic center, community college, senior citizens' center or service organization. The YMCA and YWCA often provide a variety of programs, including exercise classes specifically for older adults.

For further information on exercise programs, write to:

National Institute on Aging
Information Center/Exercise
P.O. Box 8057
Gaithersburg, MD 20898-8057

APPENDIX I

Preventing Accidents
and Falls

Because of the physical limitations that sometimes accompany age, older people tend to be more likely to suffer from accidents than their younger counterparts. As I noted within the body of this book, people over 65 take in 12 percent of the total population of the United States, but they account for 27 percent of all accidental deaths. Attention to safety measures can prevent many of these accidents.

The National Institute on Aging (NIA) has offered the following information to help older people prevent accidents.[1]

Falls

According to the NIA, falls are the most common cause of fatal injury for older people. Earlier in this book, in chapters on living independently and on moving in with family members, I discussed ways to accident proof a home. In addition, the NIA offers these practical suggestions to help you accident proof the everyday activities enjoyed by you or your elderly loved one.

- Have your vision and hearing tested regularly. If your doctor finds a problem or deficiency, make sure it is properly corrected.

- Check with your doctor or pharmacist about the side effects of any prescribed or over-the-counter medications you are taking. You may find that they will affect your coordination and balance. Ask your doctor or pharmacist if he or she knows of any ways to reduce your risk of falling.

- Limit your intake of alcohol. Even a little may affect already impaired balance and reflexes.

- Be careful about standing up too quickly after you have been eating, lying down, or resting. Low blood pressure at these times may cause dizziness.

- Keep the night-time temperature in your home set on at least 65 degrees Fahrenheit. Prolonged exposure to cold may cause your body temperature to drop, leading to dizziness.

- Use a cane, walking stick, or even a walker to maintain your balance on uneven ground, particularly if you sometimes feel dizzy. Be especially careful on wet, icy, or otherwise slippery pavement.

- Wear rubber-soled or low-heeled shoes. Try not to walk on stairs or on waxed floors with just slippers or socks on your feet, as they increase your chances of slipping.

- Maintain a regular exercise program. Regular physical activity will improve your strength and muscle tone, increasing your flexibility.

Burns

Burns are particularly harmful to older people, whose recovery from burns tends to be slow. The following list of safety measures will help you or your elderly loved one to prevent fires and burns.

- Never smoke in bed. Better yet, quit smoking altogether.

- Don't wear loose fitting clothing, such as bedclothes, when you are cooking.

- Set your water heater thermostat at a low enough temperature that the hot water will not scald your skin.

- Plan emergency procedures in case of fire—make sure you know which exit you will use. Install locks that can be opened quickly from inside your home to enable you to get out quickly.

- Use caution with all of your appliances, but be especially careful with space heaters.

Motor Vehicle Accidents

According to the NIA, motor vehicle accidents are the most common cause of accidental death among people age 65 to 74, and the second most common among older people in general. An elderly person's ability to drive may be impaired by age-related changes such as limited night vision and slowed reflexes. You can, however, compensate for some of these changes. If you are impaired but still competent to drive legally:

- Drive on familiar roads and avoid driving at night.

- Plan routes that avoid left-hand turns at busy intersections.

- Use caution when parking. If possible, park in places where you don't need to back up.

- Always wear your seat belt.

- If you are driving on toll roads, keep your change in a certain, handy place in your car. This practice will help you to avoid the temptation to fumble for money while you are driving.

For additional information about personal safety or for classes in defensive driving, refer to Appendix D. It includes a listing of agencies that offer driver safety programs or information. Or you may want to refer additional questions to:

The National Institute on Aging
Public Information Office
National Institutes of Health
9000 Rockville Pike
Building 31, Room 5C27
Bethesda, MD 20892
301-496-1752

APPENDIX J

Crime Prevention for the Elderly

Regarding con artists, the late Helen Hayes once noted, "Experience may be the best teacher, but *you* don't have to be the guinea pig."[1] That's wise advice to older people, and it doesn't apply just to the con game, but to all forms of crime.

According to the National Institute on Aging (NIA), "one of the biggest worries shared by older people is that they might be victims of violent crime." In reality, violent crimes such as murder, rape, and assault have a low rate of occurrence among elders. But other crimes, such as purse snatching, fraud, theft of checks in the mail, vandalism, and harassment affect a lot of senior citizens. And for many, the fear of crime can be as harmful as the crime itself, for worry over a long period of time can impact a person's physical and mental health.[2]

In Your Home

The following suggestions, provided by the NIA, will help you or your elderly loved one to prevent crime in the home. Some of them may seem a little elementary, but reviewing them may at least alleviate some worry.

- Lock your doors and windows. When someone knocks or rings your doorbell, look through the peephole or ask the visitor to identify himself before you open the door.

- Mark valuable property by engraving it with your driver's license or state identification number. For items that are hard to engrave, take photos and keep them, along with a list of your valuables, in a safe-deposit box.

- Install good security equipment on locks, doors, and windows. You may find that your local police department will send a representative to your home to evaluate what you have and make suggestions for alterations.

Away from Home

When you are away from home, perhaps even just walking in your neighborhood, stay alert. If possible, ask a friend or relative to go with you, or make use of an escort service as described in the section on home health care in Chapter 5. Avoid areas that are not well lit. Also, consider the following suggestions:

- Don't dress in a "showy" manner. Leave any furs or flashy jewelry, even if it is just costume jewelry, in a safe place. A thief probably can't tell the difference between fake and real—and he or she might not care, anyway.

- If you are confronted by a robber, hand over your cash without question.

- If at all possible, don't carry a purse. Keep your money and credit cards or wallet in an inside pocket of your clothing. This is the easiest way to avoid being the victim of a pickpocket or a purse snatcher. However, if you feel you *must* carry a purse, never carry it loosely. Hold it close to your body. Even if it has a shoulder strap, keep your hand on the purse, preferably at the lock. Finally, it's a good idea to keep an inventory of the items in your purse. That way, if anything is stolen, you can report it exactly to the police, and you can more easily collect from your insurance company. Make sure you have clear identification in your purse so that if it is found, it can be returned to you.

- Perhaps you will want to have your monthly pension or Social Security checks deposited directly into your bank account to avoid their being stolen in the mail.

Scams

You can avoid being "taken" in scams or con games. Scams are attempts to swindle someone out of money, property, or other valuable possessions. For instance, a con artist may call you on the phone, posing as an employee from the telephone company. He may tell you he believes someone has stolen the number from your phone card, and he simply is calling to verify your number. Then, he may ask you what your number is.

In such a situation, you should refuse to give him your number over the phone. You may want to thank him for giving you this information, and tell him you will call the telephone company immediately and let them know the situation. But don't give your phone card number, or any credit card number for that matter, to a stranger who calls you on the telephone and requests it.

The NIA also offers this example of a con game that may be used against the elderly. A con artist may pose as a bank examiner and request that you withdraw money from your bank account and turn it over to him "temporarily." He may even try to convince you that this is a "test" the bank is conducting to root out a dishonest employee. Don't fall for this type of scam. Don't ever withdraw money from your account at the suggestion or request of a stranger.

According to the NIA, the following are some common schemes you should watch for:

- Health insurance policies that claim to pay for gaps in Medicare coverage. Some do and some don't. Before you buy, check with your state insurance commission regarding that particular policy. Or write to the United Senior Health Cooperative for information. The address is 1331 H Street, NW, Suite 500, Washington, DC 20005.

- Glasses or hearing aids sold at reduced rates by unlicensed dealers. Ask your doctor's advice regarding any such product.

- Products advertised as miracle cures for everything from arthritis to cancer to baldness to insomnia. Avoid buying products that promise to treat a condition for which medical science has not yet found a cure.

- Contributions to charity. Make sure your donations go to legitimate organizations.

- Investment opportunities that seem to be "too good to be true"—they probably are. If you are considering withdrawing a large sum of money from your bank account for such a venture, I suggest that you discuss the proposal with a representative from your bank.

- Home repair frauds. Don't agree to have work done by someone who is "just passing through." Shop around and get a few estimates before you embark on any remodeling or home improvement projects.

- Door-to-door salesmen who pressure you to make an immediate purchase. If you have any hesitation at all regarding the product, but still you are a little interested, ask the person to come back another day. This will give you an opportunity to check out an unfamiliar company by calling the Better Business Bureau.

Finally, if you are victimized in some criminal way, make sure you report the crime to the proper authorities. At the very least, your report will help to ensure better protection in the future for you and others like you. If you need legal assistance, refer to Appendix E, which lists legal resources available to the elderly.

For additional information, contact:

American Association of Retired Persons (AARP)
601 E Street, NW
Washington, DC 20049
202-434-AARP (202-434-2277)

Council of Better Business Bureaus
4200 Wilson Boulevard, 8th Floor
Arlington, VA 22209

Food and Drug Administration
Center for Devices and Radiological Health
(HFZ-210)
5600 Fishers Lane
Rockville, MD 20857

APPENDIX K

A Medical
Who's Who

Many older Americans are finding that the family doctor is no longer their sole provider of medical care and advice. The variety of health needs evidenced in our culture has given birth to a variety of health providers and specialists. According to the National Institute on Aging, "it is important to understand which professionals can offer the best and least costly care for a specific problem and which services normally will be paid by Medicare."

The following is a list of definitions for different types of health care professionals who may be called on to treat elderly patients. These definitions were provided by the NIA.[1]

Physician Care

Doctors of medicine (M.D.) use all accepted methods of medical care. They treat diseases and injuries, provide preventive care, do routine checkups, prescribe drugs, and do some surgery. M.D.s complete medical school plus three to seven years of graduate medical education. They must be licensed by the state in which they practice.

Doctors of osteopathic medicine (D.O.) provide general health care to individuals and families. The training osteopaths receive is similar to that of medical doctors. In addition to treating patients with drugs, surgery, and other treatments, a D.O. may emphasize movement in treating problems of muscles, bones, and joints.

Family practitioners are M.D.s or D.O.s who specialize in providing comprehensive, continuous health care for all family members, regardless of age or sex.

Geriatricians are physicians with special training in the diagnosis, treatment, and prevention of disorders in older people. Geriatric medicine recognizes aging as a normal process, not a disease state.

Internists (M.D. or D.O.) specialize in the diagnosis and medical treatment of diseases in adults.

Surgeons treat diseases, injuries, and deformities by operating on the body. A general surgeon is qualified to perform many common operations, but many specialize in one area of the body. For example, **neurosurgeons** treat disorders relating to the nervous system, spinal cord, and brain; **orthopedic surgeons** treat disorders of the bones, joints, muscles, ligaments, and tendons; and **thoracic surgeons** treat disorders of the chest.

The physicians listed above may refer patients to any of the following specialists:

- *Cardiologist*—heart specialist.

- *Dermatologist*—skin specialist.

- *Endocrinologist*—specializing in disorders of the glands of internal secretion (diabetes, for example).

- *Gastroenterologist*—specializing in diseases of the digestive tract.

- *Gerontologist*—specializing in aging and the problems associated with it.

- *Gynecologist*—specializing in the women's reproductive system.

- *Hematologist*—specializing in blood disorders.

- *Nephrologist*—specializing in kidney diseases.

- *Neurologist*—specializing in disorders of the nervous system.

- *Oncologist*—cancer treatment specialist.

- *Ophthalmologist*—eye specialist.

- *Otolaryngologist*—specializing in diseases of the ear, nose, and throat.

- *Physiatrist*—specializing in physical medicine and rehabilitation.

- *Psychiatrist*—specializing in mental, emotional, and behavioral disorders.

- *Pulmonary specialist*—specializing in disorders of the lungs and chest.

- *Rheumatologist*—specializing in the treatment of arthritis and rheumatism.

- *Urologist*—specializing in the urinary system for both sexes and in the male reproductive system.

Dental Care

Dentists (D.D.S. or D.M.D.) treat oral conditions such as gum disease and tooth decay. They give regular checkups and routine preventive care, such as filling cavities, removing teeth, providing dentures, and checking for cancers of the mouth. Dentists can prescribe medication and perform oral surgery.

A general dentist might refer patients to a dentist who specializes in geriatrics, or perhaps to any of the following specialists:

- *Endodontist*—an expert on root canals.

- *Oral surgeon*—an expert on difficult tooth removals and surgery on the jaw.

- *Periodontist*—an expert on gum disease.

Eye Care

Ophthalmologists (M.D. or D.O.) specialize in diagnosis and treatment of eye disease. They also prescribe glasses and contact lenses, and they can prescribe drugs and perform surgery. They often treat older people who have glaucoma and cataracts.

Also working within the field of eye care are the following practitioners:

- **Optometrists (O.D)**—trained to diagnose eye abnormalities and to prescribe, supply, and adjust eyeglasses and contact lenses. In most states, optometrists can use drugs to diagnose eye disorders. An optometrist may refer patients to an ophthalmologist or other medical specialist in cases requiring medication or surgery.

- **Opticians**—trained to fit, supply, and adjust eyeglasses and contact lenses that have been prescribed by an ophthalmologist or an optometrist.

Mental Health Care

Psychiatrists (M.D. or D.O.) treat people with mental and emotional difficulties. They can prescribe medication and counsel patients and can perform diagnostic tests to determine physical problems.

Psychologists (Ph.D., Psy.D., Ed.D., or M.A.) are trained and licensed to assess, diagnose, and treat people with mental, emotional, or behavioral disorders. They counsel people through individual, group, or family therapy.

Nursing Care

Registered nurses (R.N.) have two to four years of education in nursing school. In addition to giving medicine, administering treatments, and educating patients in hospitals, R.N.s also provide these services in doctors' offices, clinics, and community health agencies.

Nurse practitioners (R.N. or N.P.) are registered nurses with training beyond basic nursing education. They perform physical examinations and diagnostic tests, counsel patients, and develop treatment programs. They may work independently, such as in rural clinics, or they may be staff members at hospitals and other health facilities. They are educated in a number of specialties, including gerontological nursing.

Licensed practical nurses (L.P.N.) have from twelve to eighteen months of training and are most frequently found in hospitals and long-term care facilities, where they provide much of the routine patient care. They also assist physicians and registered nurses.

Rehabilitation

Occupational therapists (O.T.) help patients whose ability to function has been impaired by accident, illness, or other disability. They increase or restore independence in feeding, bathing, dressing, homemaking, and social experiences through specialized activities designed to improve function.

Physical therapists (P.T.) help people whose strength, movement, or sensation is impaired. They may use exercise; heat, cold, or water therapy; or other treatments to control pain, strengthen muscles, and improve coordination.

Speech-language pathologists may work with **audiologists**. Both specialists evaluate patients and provide treatment to restore as much normal function as possible. Many speech-language pathologists work with stroke victims, people who have had their vocal cords removed, or those who have developmental speech and language disorders. Audiologists work with people who have difficulty hearing. They may recommend and dispense hearing aids.

General Care

Pharmacists are knowledgeable about the chemical makeup and correct use of medicines. They have legal authority to dispense drugs according to formal instructions issued by physicians, dentists, or podiatrists. They also can provide information on nonprescription products sold in pharmacies.

Physician assistants (P.A.) generally work in hospitals or doctors' offices. They perform some tasks traditionally done by doctors, such as taking medical histories and doing physical examinations. P.A.s must always be under the supervision of a doctor.

Podiatrists (D.P.M.) diagnose, treat, and prevent diseases and injuries to the foot. They perform surgery, make devices to correct or prevent foot problems, provide toenail care, and prescribe certain drugs.

Registered dietitians (R.D.) provide nutrition care, services, and counseling. Most work in hospitals, public health agencies, or doctors' offices, but some are in private practice. *Nutritionist* is a broader title used by a wide range of professionals, including some R.D.s. Those who wish to practice under that title possibly have not fulfilled licensing or certification requirements. Before seeking the advice of a health practitioner in nutrition, it may be wise to ask about his or her training and practical experience.

Social workers in health care settings pursue community services for patients. They provide counseling when necessary, and they help patients and their families handle problems related to physical and mental illness and disability. Frequently they coordinate the multiple aspects of care related to illness, including discharge planning from hospitals.

According to the NIA, these and other health professionals are especially important to older adults, some of whom require a great deal of specialized medical attention. For additional resources on health and aging, feel free to write to the NIA Information Center at 9000 Rockville Pike, Building 31, Room 5C27, Bethesda, MD 20892, or call 301-496-1752.

NOTES

Introduction

1. Martin A. Janis, *The Joys of Aging* (Dallas, TX: Word Publishing, 1988), 15.
2. Helen Hayes, with Marion Glasserow Gladney, *Our Best Years* (Garden City, NY: Doubleday, 1984), xi, xiv.
3. Janis, *The Joys of Aging,* 9.
4. Sherwood Wirt, "I Don't Know What Old Is, But Old Is Older Than Me," *A Better Tomorrow,* Premiere Issue, 31–32, 34–35.
5. U.S. Bureau of the Census, *Statistical Abstract of the United States: 1992* (112th edition), Washington, DC, 123.
6. Janis, *The Joys of Aging,* 35.

Chapter 1: The Best Way

1. Ken Dychtwald and Joe Fowler, *Age Wave* (Los Angeles, CA: Jeremy P. Tarcher, Inc., 1989), 106–107.
2. Ibid, 104.
3. Ibid, 100.
4. Proverbs 16:31, THE NEW KING JAMES VERSION. Copyright © 1979, 1980, 1982, Thomas Nelson, Inc., Publishers.

NOTES

Chapter 2: It's Off to Work We Go

1. William Fry Jr., "Humor, Physiology, and the Aging Process," in *Humor and Aging*, eds. Lucille Nahemow, Kathleen A. McCluskey Fawcett, and Paul E. McGhee (Orlando, FL: Academic Press, Inc., Harcourt Brace Jovanovich, 1986), 81-98.

2. Garson Kanin, *It Takes a Long Time to Become Young* (Garden City, NY: Doubleday, 1978), 150.

3. Arthur Liebers, *How to Start a Profitable Retirement Business* (Babylon, NY: Pilot Industries, Inc., 1985, 1987 edition), 7.

4. Kanin, *It Takes a Long Time to Become Young*, 171-172.

5. Liebers, *How to Start a Profitable Retirement Business*, 9.

6. "Mind Over Medicine," *The Virginian-Pilot and Ledger-Star*, 29 March 1993, B-3.

7. Joan C. Stanus, "A tough job: (she loved it): Woman finds peace recruiting for the corps," *The Compass* (Norfolk, VA), 31 March/1 April 1993, 3.

8. Kanin, *It Takes a Long Time to Become Young*, 148-149.

Chapter 3: Taking Charge

1. Norman Cousins, *The Healing Heart: Antidotes to Panic and Helplessness* (New York, NY: W.W. Norton & Company, 1983), 25-29, 35, 43-44, 49-50, 158, 235.

Chapter 4: A Family Affair

1. Charles Taylor, ed., *Growing On: Ideas About Aging* (New York, NY: Van Nostrand Reinhold Company, Inc., 1984), 97.

2. Tim Stafford, *As Our Years Increase—Loving, Caring, Preparing: A Guide* (Grand Rapids, MI: Pyranees Books, Zondervan Publishing House, 1989), 12.

3. Stephen Sapp, *Full of Years: Aging and the Elderly in the Bible and Today* (Nashville, TN: Abingdon Press, 1987), 45-47.

4. Ibid.

5. Melinda Beck, with Barbara Kantrowitz, Lucille Beachy, Mary Hagee, Jeanne Gordon, Elizabeth Roberts, and Roxie Hammill, "Trading Places," *Newsweek*, 16 July 1990, 48-49.

6. Barbara Silverstone and Helen Kandel Hyman, *You & Your Aging Parents* (New York, NY: Pantheon Books, 1976, 1982), 43-49.

7. Frances Leonard, "Home Alone," *Modern Maturity*, December 1992/January 1993, 46-51, 77.

Chapter 5: Home, Sweet Home

1. Silverstone and Hyman, *You & Your Aging Parents*, 135-137.

2. Taylor, *Growing On: Ideas About Aging*, 14.

3. Patricia H. Rushford, *The Help, Hope, and Cope Book for People with Aging Parents* (Old Tappan, NJ: Fleming H. Revell Co., 1985, 1993), 68-71.

4. Taylor, *Growing On: Ideas About Aging*, 19-20.

Chapter 6: Moving In with the Kids

1. Jo Horne, *Caregiving: Helping an Aging Loved One* (Glenview, IL: Scott, Foresman and Company, and the American Association of Retired Persons, 1985), 43.

2. Ibid, 49–50.

3. Ibid, 43–44.

4. Ibid, 49–50.

5. Ibid, 43–44.

6. Elaine Brody, *Women in the Middle: Their Parent-Care Years* (New York, NY: Springer Publishing Company, Inc., 1990), 41–45.

7. Rhonda J. V. Montgomery and Joyce Prothero. eds., *Developing Respite Services for the Elderly* (Seattle, WA: University of Washington Press, 1986), 36.

Chapter 7: Home Away from Home

1. Ruth von Behren, "Adult Day Care: A Decade of Growth," *Perspective on Aging*, July/August 1989, 14–17.

2. Mildred Beck, with Vicki Quade, Elizabeth Roberts, Jeanne Gordon, and Peter Anin, "A Home Away from Home," *Newsweek*, 2 July 1990, 56–58.

3. von Behren, "Adult Day Care: A Decade of Growth," 14–17.

4. Ibid.

5. "An Adult Day Care Chronology," *Perspective on Aging*, July/August 1989, 18.

6. *National Institute on Adult Day Care Position Paper— Adult Day Care: A Treatment Program for Persons with Functional Impairment*, 1991, 2.

7. Ibid.

8. von Behren, "Adult Day Care: A Decade of Growth," 14–17.

9. Carol Lawson, "Day Care Offers a Better Life to the

Old and Ill," *New York Times*, 20 August 1992, C-1, C-10.

10. Beck, Quade, Roberts, Gordon, and Anin, "A Home Away from Home," 56-58.

11. Ibid.

12. Pat Moore, *Disguised* (Waco, TX: Word Books, 1985), 144, 150.

13. Teresa Manfredi and Robert K. Jenkins, eds., *What's Working in Adult Day Care* (Wall Township, NJ: Health Resources Publishing, 1989), 64-70.

14. Barbara Kantrowitz, with Lauren Picker, "Daycare: Bridging the Generation Gap, *Newsweek*, 16 July 1990, 52.

Chapter 8: Facts and Myths of Dementia

1. Taylor, *Growing On: Ideas About Aging,* 69.

2. "Alzheimer's Disease: An Overview," pamphlet available from the Alzheimer's Disease and Related Disorders Association, Inc., 919 N. Michigan Ave., Suite 1000, Chicago, IL 60611-1676.

3. Charles Leroux, *Coping and Caring: Living with Alzheimer's Disease* (Washington, DC: American Association of Retired Persons, in cooperation with the Alzheimer's Disease and Related Disorders Association, Inc., 1991), 3.

4. Donna Cohen and Carl Eisdorfer, M.D., *The Loss of Self: A Family Resource for the Care of Alzheimer's Disease and Related Disorders* (New York, NY: W. W. Norton & Company, 1986), 33-34.

5. Ibid, 12.

6. Leonard Heston, M.D., and June White, *Dementia: A Practical Guide to Alzheimer's Disease* (New York, NY: W. H. Freeman and Company, 1983), 25-26, 29-32.

7. "Alzheimer's Disease: An Overview," pamphlet from the Alzheimer's Disease and Related Disorders Association, Inc.

8. Lenore S. Powell, Ed.D., and Katie Courtice, *Alzheimer's Disease: A Guide for Families* (Reading, MA: Addison-Wesley Publishing Company, 1983, 1993) 159-161, 163-164, 166-172.

Chapter 12: The Future Is Serious

1. Harry R. Moody, *Ethics in an Aging Society* (Baltimore, MD: The Johns Hopkins University Press, 1992), 1-2.

2. Robert N. Butler, "The Effects of Medical and Health Progress on the Social and Economic Aspects of the Lifestyle," paper to the National Institute of Industrial Gerontologists, 1969.

3. Robert N. Butler, "Dispelling Ageism: The Cross-Cutting Intervention," *The Annals of the American Academy of Political and Social Science*, May 1989.

Appendix H

1. Jane E. Brody, "Healthy Words to Live By," *Modern Maturity,* October/November 1988.

Appendix I
1. This information comes from an "Age Page" titled "Accident Prevention," available from the National Institute on Aging.

Appendix J
1. Hayes with Gladney, *Our Best Years,* 17.
2. This information comes from an "Age Page" titled "Crime and Older People," available from the National Institute on Aging.

Appendix K
1. This information comes from an "Age Page" titled "Who's Who in Health Care," available from the National Institute on Aging.

INDEX

See also chore services; emergency response systems; escort and transportation services; Meals on Wheels

longevity revolution, 9–10

lung and respiratory disease, 265

Ma, Yo-Yo, 29

McDaniel, Geneva, 65

Mace, Nancy L., 164

Man Who Laughed Himself Well, The (Cousins), 54

Matisse, Henri, 17

maturian, 6, 215

Meals on Wheels, 99–100

Medicaid, 93, 98, 103, 137, 170, 176–178, 204, 207, 217–218

Medic-Alert, 162, 265

Medicare, 92, 93, 98, 99, 103, 170, 177–178, 204, 207, 267, 316

Medicare/Medicaid Anti-Fraud Abuse Amendments, 204–205

Menninger, Roy, M.D., 153

mental disability. *See* dementia

Mental Health Associations, 234

minerals, dietary, 283

misconceptions about elderly, 2–4, 7–8, 29–30, 49–50, 68. *See also* stereotypes of elderly

Moody, Harry R., 222–223, 226

Moore, Pat, 147–148

Mother Teresa, 18, 160–161

motor vehicle accidents, prevention of, 307–308

National Association for Home Care, 70, 133

National Association of Area Agencies on Aging, 37–38, 97, 254

National Association of Private Geriatric Care Managers, 82–83. *See also* geriatric care

National Association of State Units on Aging (NASUA), 236–249

National Council of Senior Citizens, 254

National Council on the Aging, 7, 254